FREEDOM, ANARCHY, AND THE LAW

Second Edition

Freedom, Anarchy, and the Law

An Introduction to Political Philosophy
Second Edition

Richard Taylor

P̃ Prometheus Books

700 East Amherst Street
Buffalo, N.Y. 14215

Originally published 1973
by Prentice-Hall, Inc.
Englewood Cliffs, New Jersey

Reprinted in 1980
by Linden Books
Interlaken, New York

Published 1982 by Prometheus Books
700 East Amherst Street, Buffalo, New York 14215

Library of Congress Number 82-80179
ISBN 0-87975-176-2

Printed in the United States of America

To My Dear Mother

CONTENTS

PREFACE TO THE SECOND EDITION

When this book first appeared, in 1973, it was greeted by philosopher John Hospers and others as a contribution to libertarian political philosophy, even though the word *libertarian* did not appear in it. I had not thought of the ideas embodied in my book as expressing libertarian principles, and yet I could hardly fail to see the aptness of Hospers's observations.

It will be desirable here, then, to place this book within the libertarian framework, and also to note two areas where my ideas do not match those of some of the leading libertarians. These concern the importance of private property and the concept of natural rights. The central idea of my book is one that is basic to libertarianism, namely, that the interests of modern governments, including those democratically chosen, and the powerful interest groups they must heed, are often antithetical to the best and noblest interests of individuals.

The philosophical problem. The basic task of contemporary political philosophy in a free society is to formulate principles for the protection of individuals from the titanic power of the masses and of the government that often speaks for them. That power no longer expresses itself primarily by the sword, although of course government's ability to enforce its will by threat is always there. What is more insidious is the sheer growth of government and its inherent tendency to expand and spread itself out like flowing lava into a suffocating bureaucracy that reaches into every aspect of our individual lives. Ordinary people, that is, people who are for the most part without ideas of their own, swarm about this leviathan, nourished by a public treasury, as flies swarm about and cling to a rotting carcass. Meanwhile those gifted individuals, always in the minority, who strike out for themselves with their own ideas and values, and with the intelligence, courage, and creativity that the ancients called *virtue,* must sometimes struggle to breathe. Our democratic and egalitarian traditions, as well as our religious traditions, reinforce this baneful tendency, teaching that the least among us is just as good as the best, and therefore just as deserving, at whatever cost. The welfare state and all its heavy machinery is the logical outcome of this view. Worse yet, the virtue of the vulgar, who usually conceive of no loftier view of life than what is embodied in church, flag, and family, is held up as the virtue for all, and every politician tries to outdo the others in declaring his dedication to those wretched ideals.

The double threat. Government, or, more generally, organized society, presents two quite different kinds of threats to individual freedom. The first is inherent in government itself, that is, in the rule of the many by the few. The second, on the other hand, is posed just by the pressures of social life itself.

With respect to the first of these, government "by the people," or self-government, literally construed, can logically only mean no government at all, as philosophical anarchists have clearly seen. No one can be governed by others, even to the smallest degree, and still be entirely self-governing, or autonomous. But the rule of the many by the few must in the nature of the case depend upon force. If large numbers of persons are to be expected to do what they would not voluntarily do, and simply at the behest of a smaller number who hold the power of government, then that expectation can be no stronger than the power of the latter to compel obedience. Why else are the agents of government, at that ultimate point where habit or persuasion has failed, always armed?

Political philosophers, and particularly those who share libertarian ideals, have usually been thoroughly aware of the dangers to freedom embodied in this model. They have sought to reduce the danger in various ways, some mild, some extreme. Thus the guarantees of liberty embodied in the U.S. Constitution are much promoted by some, and test cases are sometimes arranged in order to achieve a protection of those liberties by the courts. The freedom to disseminate contraceptives and information pertaining to them, now quite taken for granted, was finally solidified in just this way (*Griswold* vs. *Connecticut,* 1965). A more far-reaching way of dealing with the danger has been the attempt to reduce the power of government by restricting its power to tax. Another has been the effort, by now largely but not entirely successful, to eliminate all "victimless crime" from the criminal statutes. More radical, but with the same end in view, has been the attempt, through philosophical writing and political tract, to reduce the role and functions of government, even to the point of zero, as represented in the small but significant literature of anarchism. It is in this area, of course, that philosophy has played a significant role, particularly through the writings of libertarians.

Libertarians are agreed that it is no business of government to lead us upon the path of virtue, as Plato, together with every priest and cleric, would have it do. Immorality cannot, as such, be prosecuted as a crime. The condemnation of it must be verbal only, this being the traditional role of the church. Thus the attempt to

compel women, by the threat of criminal sanctions, to bear misbegotten and unwanted children, as advocated by those who misleadingly call themselves "pro-life," is
anathema to anyone with the smallest sense of individual liberty. The same partisans
of elementary human freedoms will of course condemn any attempt by government
to compel loveless couples to remain legally married, or to determine what people
may read or look at, even in the privacy of their homes, or to decide for them what
they may or may not do or purchase on the sabbath, and so on.

But it is likewise, in the eyes of libertarians, no business of government to pour
blessings upon us in the form of art, "health care" (as it is called), safety from our
own freely chosen actions, and so on. Anarchists carry this reduction to its logical
extreme, and it is the task of any political philosophy to find, along the continuum
thus created, that role of government which is least incompatible with freedom and
at the same time adequate to the basic needs of protection. *Any* government represents a compromise with freedom, and *no* government can protect us from all
danger. So we have to seek the most we can of these incompatible ends, at least cost.
That was the main purpose of my book, and it seems to me that it was achieved.

The societal threat. The second threat is not so much to the individual as to
individuality itself, and it is posed not by government but by society, often much
reinforced by the power and prestige of government.

Thus the church is not in most Western nations an arm of government; yet
those who speak for it have behind them the power of masses of people, and their
invariant purpose is to grind down the opponents of their principles to conformity,
through legislation wherever possible. Even in the absence of the assistance of the
police and the judicial system, however, the force such groups exert is constant, like
gravity, which it also resembles in exerting a constant pressure downwards. It is
never uplifting—except, of course, in the eyes of the church, which sees the common, the banal, the customary, the traditional, and the narrow as being one and the
same as the moral.

That the defenders of this or that morality or religion should be free to speak
anywhere, anytime, and to anyone is of course not to be questioned. Nor does anyone in a modern democracy seriously question the right of their foes to the very same
freedom. The threat to freedom lies rather in the power of such persons not merely
to speak but to exert an influence over government, and over legislation, far out of
proportion to the numerical strength of the movements they represent. This has
resulted largely from the growth of television and from computerized methods of
rallying vast numbers of people behind a single issue, and summoning up, at the
push of a button, staggering sums of money for the furtherance of isolated schemes.
And the efforts of such persons are not merely to get their doctrines *heard,* but, with
the help of government, to get them *imposed.*

Of course the problem here is not merely that such spokesmen do not speak for
all, or even, usually, for a majority. Their efforts would be evil even if they had the
total support of everyone, for this would render the very idea of individuality un-
thinkable. Thus it is not really a question of majority rule. Whether or not such

forces for morality happen to speak for a majority, or even an overwhelming majority, or even a totality, is beside the point. It is a question, instead, of whether society has any legitimate role in the enforcement of morality at all. Nor is it simply a question of individual freedom. It is a matter of preserving a social atmosphere in which individuality itself can flourish, something that is often difficult even in those societies that are politically most free and benignly governed. The pressure to *conform*, which is always the pressure to conform to what is common, established, unoriginal, and acceptable to all, is always there, whether reinforced by law or not.

In this age when every popular government is eager to speak for the masses, for the very ordinary people who of necessity constitute a majority, it has to be stressed that what is ordinary is never really good, that the common is opposed to the noble and the exceptional, and that the conventional and the accepted are always at war with the innovative and the imaginative, especially in the realm of conduct. To declare that the least and most common of persons is as good as the best is not so much to elevate the former, which is a very difficult thing to do, but rather to grind down the latter, which is, alas, quite easy.

The purpose of government. If we raise the question, Why do we need any government at all? then the answer that will justify itself is, I think: For the protection of individuals from actual injuries from others, and really very little else. That was the original thesis of my book, and I have found no reason to change it.

Notice that I say "actual injury from others," which implies two important points. The first is that it is not a proper function of any government to protect anyone from himself. And the second is that we are entitled to protection by government, not from any and all evils, but only from actual injury from other persons.

These two points are of great importance, in that both popular and theoretical political positions turn on them. In fact much of the confusion in contemporary politics results from a mingling and confusion of these ideas. They need, then, to be carefully explained.

Paternalism and freedom. Every legal restraint is a restriction upon freedom, for it prevents someone from doing what he would otherwise do. Some such restraints are, to be sure, needed for sheer safety, but they are nevertheless restraints and thus limitations upon someone's freedom of action. To what purpose, therefore, should they be imposed by government?

One principle, eloquently enunciated by J. S. Mill and reaffirmed here, is that protection of an adult and rational person *from his own actions and choices* cannot, in any coherent political philosophy, be a part of that purpose. What I do to others is a legitimate concern to others; what I freely and in full awareness of the risks do only to myself is of no proper concern to anyone but myself. It is here that every rational person having a sense of life's values will say, not just to the agents of government, but to every person or group who tries to direct his conduct: Mind your *own* business. There, within the precious realm of choice where consequences are primarily if not exclusively one's own, the individual is indeed his own sovereign. For anyone, whether clothed with the authority of government, church, or whatever, even to question that right of choice, for whatever good or even exalted purpose, is at least to meddle and at most to tyrannize. Nothing whatever can justify it, not even the proved or overwhelming harm to oneself that one courts by his own behavior.

Thus, just as it is not the place of government to fill the role of a big brother always there to assist us, neither should it function like a father seeing to it that we do what is good for ourselves and protecting us from our own folly.

There are numberless instances of failure to heed this seemingly obvious principle, many of them relatively trivial but others not. One, for example, is the mandatory inclusion on cars of various devices, such as seatbelts or airbags, for the protection of their drivers. These are installed at the command of government but at the expense of the owners. Consumer advocates who busily promote such ideas demonstrate a childish understanding of philosophical principle. It is quite irrelevant to point out, however correctly, the perhaps great loss of life that such requirements prevent, for no lives are risked by such disregard other than the lives of those who chose that very risk. One's life is one's own, to risk as one pleases. It is not something for which one is in any way beholden to others.

Similar remarks can of course be made about the use of intoxicants, health care, and the whole area of choice where the consequences of one's conduct are chiefly to oneself. And beyond this, of course, we can include the realm of behavior whose consequences are also to others, but with their own consent. Thus no sexual practices are any business of the law, or indeed of any outsider at all, so long as others are directly affected by their own consent. No considerations of morality, as such, can ever justify the invasion of the individual's realm of choice, for to choose *for* someone else, without regard to actual injury to others, is itself an ultimate immorality.

Mill's principle. These basic principles were of course formulated in Mill's essay *On Liberty,* but the vagueness of the concept of *injury* in his formulations is fatal. We can say, with Mill, that an individual is entitled to do anything he chooses short of injuring others, but how narrowly are we to construe "injury"? Does he mean only *bodily* injury? If so, then theft and fraud are rendered permissible by his formula, since neither is an injury in that narrow sense. But if the meaning of "injury" is broadened to include any effect upon others that they would deeply resent and wish to repel, such as theft and fraud, then we have thereby also included affronts to their feelings, their religious sentiments, their sense of propriety, and so on, since there certainly are people who deeply resent these and try to repel them. But then, of course, hardly anything is any longer allowable. If one cannot, for example, on Mill's own principle, so much as voice an unpopular view of religion for fear of offending the feelings of the devout, then there is obviously hardly anything left that one can do.

I tried to overcome this glaring defect by distinguishing between *natural* and *conventional* injury, suggesting that Mill's principle should apply only to injuries that people naturally resent, not those that are resented merely because of the customs and conventions imbibed from this or that culture. Many critics claimed that this modification is inadequate, however. For example, the institution of private property is a purely conventional or man-made one, and therefore violations of property rights, such as theft and fraud, appear to be mere conventional injuries after all, and thus not ruled out by my modification of Mill's principle.

The criticism is apt, but not conclusive. The *test* I proposed for distinguishing a natural from a conventional injury was whether it would be resented by virtually *any* person, regardless of his acculturation, or only by certain persons, as a direct result of their acculturation. What offends a Moslem, for example, may be inoffensive to a Christian, and something that offends an Englishman might be quite acceptable to an Eskimo. Such injuries are accordingly conventional and not prohibited under the principle of liberty that I set forth. All persons, or nearly all, resent assault, however, which is therefore a natural injury. And to this let us add that all, or nearly all, likewise resent fraud and theft, no matter how purely conventional may be the institution of property. A savage hunter regards game he has taken as *his,* and repels any effort to snatch it from him, without ever having thought of the institution of private property or its conventional foundation. And persons from Western cultures long ago learned that very different and sometimes primitive people have an acute sense of fairness, and of fraud, and that there is indeed a whole area of injury as natural to them as to anyone, quite regardless of custom.

I do believe, then, that my modification of Mill's principle is correct and workable, understood in this general but fairly clear way. If so, then I believe it does provide an important criterion for the limit that any government, or the agents of any government, or society, or any social group, or in fact any person whatever, must observe in presuming to restrict the range of another's behavior—provided, of course, that the idea of *a free people* is to have any real meaning.

The different kinds of injuries. The other point I said is implied in the words "actual injury from others" is that free people are entitled to protection by government, not from *all* injuries, whether natural or other, but only injuries *from other persons.* Illness and poverty are evils, for example, but it is not the primary business of government, and probably no proper business of government at all, to protect us from them, except insofar as they may be inflicted by others. Thus a person with a serious contagious infection may be prevented from transmitting it to others, even at the expense of his own freedom, but a free people should not turn to government for the banishment of disease itself. They should turn instead to the medical profession, and to those institutions, such as universities, upon which that profession rests. Similarly, a government may protect one from becoming impoverished by fraud and deception; but it is not the primary business of government, and probably no business of government at all, to save each and every citizen from want. Free people depend primarily upon themselves for this and can expect from government only that it will maintain those economic and social conditions, such as free competition, that make escape from poverty realistically possible. A clear instance of an appropriate governmental role here is the prevention of monopolies.

Thus the role of government, in a free society, must be essentially negative.

It exists to *prevent* certain conditions from arising, these conditions being the product of injurious behavior on the part of persons. It does not exist to eliminate all evils, nor to heap blessings upon us. In fact, government is itself an evil, but one that is absolutely necessary, simply for the prevention of that greater evil that Thomas Hobbes graphically characterized as a "war of all against all." Where government steps beyond this, then it oversteps, improperly assuming the role not merely of government but of parent and church, the first being the guardian against mundane evil, and the second the guardian of morals.

The power of government. If government exerts power legitimately only in the prevention of injury from others, then the question of the limits of that power arises. Since government, by its very nature, can summon immense force, just what is it entitled to do for the sake of protection?

I believe the only rational answer to this is that it is entitled to do *whatever is necessary.* Thus it may imprison someone who is a threat to the safety of others, and for as long as he remains a threat, even though this represents the total deprivation of the liberty of that person. But by the same token, it may not properly imprison or otherwise interfere with anyone who constitutes no such threat, however offensive that person's actions may be from the standpoint of morality. Hence punishment for wrongdoing, as such, and without regard to a continuing threat of injury, has no place in a free society.

Again, faced with the threat of injury from the hostile forces of an enemy nation, government can do *whatever is necessary* for the protection of the nation. It can, if necessary (but not otherwise), conscript men and women without any semblance of their consent and can, if necessary, consign parts of its armed forces to almost certain destruction in the defense of the others. And it can, if necessary, confiscate private property to whatever degree is necessary, including the total seizure of everything, provided measures short of this offer no assurance of safety from the enemy.

Thus the principles of liberty are not derived from any immutable principles of justice and right, such that they will apply under any and all circumstances, but from purely utilitarian considerations. The one value that is taken for granted is the freedom of any individual to do and to be whatever he wants, but while this is an ultimate value it is not an absolute one. All good things depend upon this freedom, which is more precious even than life. And by the same token, there is nothing worth preserving in the face of a threat to it.

Concerning property and natural right. I said at the outset that there are two things much lauded in the literature of libertarianism about which my ideas are not in agreement. One is the right of property, and the other a natural right to one's life. In fact the two are connected, for the right to own property is thought to derive from the right to life, property being a means to life.

But, precious as life is, I believe there exists no natural right to it. Indeed, the very idea is metaphysical, if not theological. For from what can such a right be derived if not either from some presumed metaphysical nature of man (since animals are presumed to have no such right) or from his creator? Certainly the idea is without scientific or even empirical foundation. Nor need we assume any such right as the foundation of social and political freedom. All that is needed for this, as I hope I have shown in the pages that follow, is the distinction between *good* and *bad,* which is ultimately a distinction of the will, or, in other words, one based upon human psychology.

The presupposition of a natural right to life, besides offering a very weak and shadowy foundation for liberty and a free society, has had two very baneful consequences in libertarian philosophy. For one, it quite absurdly appears to endow the fertilized human egg with that right, since such a being is without a doubt human, and alive. But in doing so it not only exposes libertarian philosophy to ridicule, it also threatens the most basic kind of freedom that libertarians have traditionally wanted to defend. For it is a logical consequence of this that the state may compel even impoverished and ignorant women to bear misbegotten and unwanted children, in total disregard of the demographic effects of this, and, more important, in disregard of the most elementary freedom that any woman can in a free society be presumed to have.

And the second baneful consequence has been the supposition that, ownership of property being thought by some to be a natural right, one is therefore entitled to possess it in any amount whatsoever, an inference much approved, of course, by the rich. And the difficulty with this is that the emphasis is all wrong. The lovers of wealth are not always lovers of liberty. The two indeed have little in common. So, by placing their emphasis upon this presumed right of property, and with it, some presumed right to wealth on the part of the wealthy, libertarians risk appearing as spokesmen for what the masses of people can only view as privilege. Indeed, I would maintain, at least for the sake of argument, that it would be perfectly consistent with every basic principle of freedom to have government confiscate by taxation every bit of private wealth above a certain fairly generous limit. This is not, of course, something that I would recommend, in the name of liberty, but it would at least tend to focus attention on what liberty really is and prevent its confusion with the simple freedom to amass wealth.

There is no proving that freedom is a precious thing, or that there is nothing more worthwhile. Indeed, it is possible that people may someday all live in ant-hill-like societies, bereft of any semblance of freedom but secure in everything else, and that they might rejoice in that condition. Such in fact seems to be more or less the ideal aimed at by some political philosophies, strangely called radical. But as long as people speak of freedom as an ideal, then it is certainly worthwhile understanding what it is, and how it is surrendered. I hope that my book contributes to that understanding.

R.T.

21 August 1981

PREFACE

These chapters grew out of the R. Hawley Truax Lectures, which were delivered to the students and faculties of Hamilton and Kirkland Colleges in April, 1971. The Truax Professorship was established at Hamilton in 1956 through the generosity of Mr. Truax, in honor of his father, Chauncey S. Truax. Both father and son were devoted alumni of the college, and throughout his career in law, publishing, and journalism, and his close association with *The New Yorker* magazine, Mr. Truax maintained a deep love for philosophy.

I wish to express my thanks to President John Chandler, Dr. Russell T. Blackwood, and the Trustees of Hamilton College for honoring me with this visiting professorship, and to Mr. Truax, whom I came to know through correspondence during the tenure of my appointment. I express also my deep gratitude to colleagues at Hamilton for their help, to Mr. John D. Moore of the Columbia University Press, and to Mr. George Coy of Prentice-Hall, Inc. for the encouragement they gave me at critical times when it was much needed.

RICHARD TAYLOR

FREEDOM, ANARCHY, AND THE LAW

The Political Animal   I

Aristotle, in a famous phrase, said that man is a "political animal," and this, rendered into English idiom, has charmed men ever since. It brings to mind the image of men busily engaged in politics, and suggests that such sophisticated and specialized behavior is the normal expression of human nature, as natural as birds nesting and spiders spinning.

But of course Aristotle meant nothing like this. He meant only to characterize men as beings who naturally live in a "polis"—that is, in a governed community. One would express exactly the same idea today by saying that men are *social* animals.

Are they? Do men gravitate into social units as the expression of their very nature? Or is social life a contrived thing, as most political theorists have supposed, something that rests on explicit or tacit agreement or compact?

Actually the truth is not very hard to discern, so long as the question being raised is not confused with others. It will be worth setting forth certain things that are fairly obvious just in order to illuminate what are considered to be the five fundamental questions of political philosophy.

The philosophical questions of government   Those five questions are: (1) What is the rational *justification* for the government of some men by others, in case any such justification exists? (2) What renders a particular governmental authority *legitimate* over those who live under it? (3) What is *good* government—that is, what is its proper end? (4) What is the proper *extent* of governmental authority over an individual? And (5) What is an individual's *duty* in his role as citizen? These five questions can, for brevity, be called the questions of (1) justification, (2) legitimacy, (3) purpose, (4) liberty, and (5) political obligation.

We shall answer all five questions. Of course they cannot be simply framed and then answered. They have to be answered in the light of certain prior considerations concerning the nature of man and of human good, and it is to these that we shall turn shortly. Meanwhile, we must make clear what the questions are, and this can best be done in terms of the questions posed by Aristotle's remark.

Reason and nature Note first, then, that the five questions raised are questions put to reason—they are philosophical questions; and second, that none of them would make sense, or even arise, if one took very seriously the opinion that Aristotle's remark seems to imply. If men were *by nature* "political," or fully social animals, then there could be no such thing as a political philosophy. This could serve to answer all the questions.

If, for example, governed associations, or the rule of large numbers of men by few, were an arrangement natural to men, then there would be no question of *justifying* it. It would be like seeking a justification for the division of mankind into male and female. One might seek an explanation in theoretical biology or even in theology, but not in philosophy. Or again, on the same supposition of the naturalness of governed societies, no question could arise concerning the proper *end* of government. One could only ask, concerning a particular governmental structure, what it is—not whether it is as it should be. Nor could one, for the same reason, sensibly ask whether a given government is *legitimate,* this being the sort of question that can be asked only of institutions created by men. And so it is with respect to all the questions of political philosophy.

Government as a human creation A political philosophy, accordingly, is possible only on the supposition that political life is a human creation. If that is the case, then we can ask of any government how it came to be, whether it is legitimate, what its purpose is and how well that purpose is served, and indeed, all the philosophical questions of government.

And that supposition does appear to be essentially correct. Men can and occasionally do live in isolation from each other, but not well. They therefore join together in order to enhance what would otherwise be an onerous and hazardous existence—an observation that gave rise, in the minds of the classical political philosophers, to the idea of a primitive "state of nature."

Some human association, to be sure, is essential even to human life; for without the elementary society represented by the family, life itself would be imperiled. The family is, in fact, a minute body politic that has all the requisite features of domain, authority, and subordination, as well as legislator, executive, and judge. Apart from size, however, it differs from a larger body politic in that, for its subjects at least, it is in no sense a voluntary association—they simply sprang from its founders. To this extent, therefore, men are by nature "political"—that is, social; for children are associated with families by nature, and not choice, and they continue this association for an indefinite time.

But now consider those larger bodies politic that one would primarily have in mind in describing men as social beings. Are men, in this context, social by nature the way they are, for example, more or less hairless by nature and unique among mammals for this? Or do they fabricate social life the way they fabricate their own clothing in that they might cast it aside without violation to their nature as men?

Social animals, apparent and real   The answer to this can be most clearly seen by comparing men to certain creatures which are, without any doubt, social by nature and not by choice. Consider bees and ants. Their life is social, *not* merely in the sense that they are found together in large numbers, but in a far deeper sense. A cloud of flies hovering over a carcass presents the spectacle of insects of a certain kind being found together in large numbers, but there is nothing in the least social in their existence. In the same way a place might be teeming with a multitude of men, without this by itself representing social life; for they might all be drawn to that place by a common attractant, or bait, like flies. Their physical proximity to each other and their large numbers are purely accidental. But in the case of a colony of bees, their physical proximity is not an accident, but on the contrary, basic to their very nature as bees. A bee, separated from its colony and confined in a bottle, is no longer a bee—just as the eye of an animal, under similar conditions, would no longer be an eye any more than the "eye" of a statue. A bee thus separated not only does none of the things characteristic of its kind, it very soon perishes. It can be a bee only as a member of a highly complex social structure. If, on the other hand, all the flies hovering over a carcass were eliminated save one, then that one would continue to function exactly as before, and perhaps even more effectively.

Of flies, accordingly, it can be said that they have no government whatever, and that their "association" is accidental and without significance. Of bees, on the other hand, we can say that their "government" is total, in that their enormously complex association is essential to their nature as bees. At the same time we recognize that the meaning of "government" is being stretched in such an application, and it is not difficult to see just how.

Political men   A society of men resembles an assemblage of flies more than a hive of bees, with this difference, that men, unlike flies, *are* governed, but unlike the case of bees, this word has a proper, nonmetaphorical meaning here. Human governments are conventional or man-made, and vary from one place to another.

Men assemble in large numbers, not only temporarily as when attending a football game, but permanently. And that which draws them together also explains the institution of government—namely, common need for each other, or aspiration to a common good, which is not merely something pursued *in common* (as in the case of flies commonly drawn to a carcass), but something pursued *in concert* (as in the case of bees working cooperatively to a common end). And surely the need to work in concert explains the emergence of government. It is simply the mechanism of common endeavor on a large scale. The goal of men living together in a "polis" may be vaguely referred to as the common good, but it is achieved not merely by living together. Government enables men to work in concert to attain what would exceed individual powers.

Men are, therefore, in terms of Aristotle's remark, political animals, not merely because they live together, which is without particular significance, but because they work together for the attainment of a common end. They are in this sense political not by nature, however, but by choice; for the means to that end, which is government, is their own creation and not a product of nature or the gods. Given this conception of political man, we can at least *ask* the basic questions of political philosophy, which we could not do if government were not of human contrivance. And given, further, some notion of what is good for man (and thereby some notion of what is the common good of any body politic), we can *answer* those very same questions. This second task is by no means as easy as the first, but with a proper approach it is far from impossible.

The Concept of Sovereignty   II

Classical political philosophers based their theories upon the idea of sovereignty. Any discourse on government that tried to proceed without this idea would have been like a treatise on astronomy that did not mention planets, or a theological treatise that omitted any reference to God.

It is no wonder, for the idea of sovereignty is one of the richest philosophical ideas men have ever created. In terms of it one can define political freedom and make intelligible what are otherwise murky questions of liberty, the limits of government, or the legitimate constraints upon lawmakers. Indeed, there is hardly any purely philosophical problem of government that does not become clearer when placed in this context.

When modern men think of sovereignty they are apt to imagine that they are dealing with an archaic notion having to do with princes and kings. This is not so. Sovereignty is the power to govern; and just as that *power* has certainly not declined with the emergence of the modern state, so also the *idea* that derives from it has lost none of its meaning and relevance.

Let us begin, then, with a consideration of this idea, in order to establish a perspective for what follows.

What sovereignty is   Every man has *by nature* one sovereign—himself. *By his faith,* if he has that gift, he acknowledges another, his creator. And *by custom and convention* he has still another, or indeed many, they

5

being all who are set over him in the political order and can subject his conduct to their will.

This last expresses the essence of sovereignty—i.e., power, or the supremacy of will. I am *subject* to whoever can bend me to his ways, and that person is, by that fact, my sovereign. So *by nature* I am sovere.gn to myself, for it is by nature and not by convention that I obey my own will. No custom, no agreement, no training, no human artifice is needed to produce that fact of sovereign and subject in one and the same person. All that is needed is that I be a man; it is not further necessary that I be a man of this or that culture, tradition, or allegiance.

Those who believe in a divine will acknowledge God as their sovereign; but this is by faith and not nature. If a man claims that God is the creator of heaven and earth, then he may also claim that God is, by that fact, supreme over all creation. The whole of it, therefore, and hence all men, must be subject to his will. But this does not make God sovereign by nature, for it is by faith that the original presupposition emerges in the first place—namely, that God is the creator of heaven and earth.

Why does the believer bow his head? And why does he kneel? Simply because these are perfect and obvious expressions of subjection. By those symbolic gestures the believer says, "Not my will, but thine." And this, in turn, is the recognition of sovereignty, or the supremacy of a will.

Thus God is not deemed sovereign by His glory or His goodness but solely by His will. One can speak of a sovereign will, whether that of God or man; but the expression "sovereign goodness" has no meaning except as an inept metaphor. Sovereignty is nothing but the supremacy of a will. It requires nothing else. And the supremacy of a will is, in turn, nothing but the subjection of the subordinate will to itself. To be compelled to do as some person, human or divine, bids is the essence of subjugation. By the same token, to be able thus to compel, according to one's own bidding, is the essence of sovereignty.

Freedom and bondage   Thus, again, is every man by nature his own sovereign and subject, his own ruler and slave. Only in one's own person is such a conjunction possible. He does as he himself bids; the will he obeys is his own. Here, and only here, is total subjugation compatible with sovereignty in one person. This also expresses the only perfect *freedom*—namely, to be subject to no will other than one's own.

The most perfect expression of *bondage,* on the other hand, is the enslavement of one man by another. What one has here is the *total* subjugation to the will of another so complete that the will of the slave, even his will to live, can be annulled by the most whimsical decree of his owner. In this picture, then, we see the exemplary specimen of sovereignty and, conversely, of subjugation; and it consists only of the supremacy of one will and the subordination of another. One is subject to, or in subjugation to, whomever he must obey. One subjects, or is sovereign over, whomever he commands. And thus we see again, in this formula, the essence of both freedom and bondage. One is free if the will in question is one's own, and in bondage if it is not.

A power of the will alone   It should be noted that sovereignty has nothing whatever to do with any quality except that of the power of a will. One is not sovereign by virtue of his goodness, wisdom, or glory, but only by his will. Thus the owner of a slave need be no *better* than his slave in any sense whatever, except what derives from the supremacy of his will. He can otherwise be more stupid, weaker, more base and corrupt. None of these faults will by itself dilute his sovereignty with respect to his slave. And so it is with any ruler. It is not essential that a ruler, if he is in fact a sovereign and not merely a figurehead, be wise or good, and certainly his sovereignty is not weakened by the discovery of subjects wiser or better. These qualities are irrelevant to the relationship.

Those who worship God do, it is true, believe Him to be superior in wisdom and goodness as well as in power. But while the former two qualities may be essential to the concept of God, they have nothing to do with His sovereignty or the idea of a divine ruler. One looks *up* to wisdom and goodness, and the believer's response to these qualities is worship and praise. On the other hand, one kneels *down* before supreme power, and the response of the believer is obedience.

The conventional corruption of freedom   We have said that by nature a man is his own sovereign power, which only means that no one is subjugated to any of his fellows by the very nature of things but only as a consequence of institutions that are created by men. Were it not for these human contrivances I would be subject to the will of no man other than myself, or at least I would only accidentally be so subject. A strong man might at any time overpower a weaker one and subject him to his will, but my subjugation to such a man would depend upon the accident of my encountering him. In a political society, on the other hand, an individual need not ever encounter those to whom he is subject; and in fact in the modern state he is not likely to. Subjugation to them depends on no fortuities but on rules and established institutions. Thus in a political society a man can be sent to his death by someone he has never seen, and who in turn may never have seen *nor heard of* him. No such relationship can be the product of nature. It can only arise from the institution of law and the machinery associated with it, all of which is of human creation.

The man who is by nature sovereign over himself is the perfect image of human freedom, and with this goes the clear and overwhelmingly important implication that men are, by nature, *free beings*. Nature presents no distinction between slave and freeman as it does between male and female, for example. Such total annulment of freedom can result only from human contrivance; a man can only be made a slave by other men. And so, likewise, with *every* dilution of the total freedom that is ours by nature. No man can by nature be subject to the will of another to any degree, even the smallest; he can, by nature, be subject only to his own. That a man can, for example, compel me to pay a tax or a fine against my own will; or that he can oblige me to risk my health or life against my will; or that in fact he can force me to do *anything*, however trivial, against my own will is no right of his by nature. If he has that right, it is by institution—that is, by convention or human artifice. He can make me pay a tax, for example, only if someone has imposed that tax; he can make me pay a fine, only if a law has been made by men whose breach is, by their decree, punishable by fine; he can make me take up arms only if, again, a law has been instituted by men that imposes certain sanctions for my refusal to obey. No one, however good he might be, however wise, or strong, or august, could ever claim that by the nature of things, and without human enactment, I owe him a tax, or a fine, or obedience, perhaps at the risk of my very life. The very idea of such a claim is laughable. It has been claimed that men owed such things to their king by the will and institution of God. But God is Himself here thought of as a person, possessed of a will, and not identical with nature; and in any case, any such suggestion made with reference to the modern state would of course be preposterous.

No one, on the other hand, would ever deny that by the very nature of things, and without human enactment, I am subject to my own will. No legislator confers upon one his power over himself. All a legislator can do is take it away—take it away completely, in the case of enslavement, or partially, as in the case of that partial bondage in which all of us live. Freedom is the gift of nature, and the compromise of it is always the work of man.

Freedom only restored, never granted   From this it can be seen that no man ever *confers* another's freedom upon him, except in the derivative sense of restoring what he had previously robbed him of. Thus a slave-owner might set his slaves free; but he would not be conferring freedom upon them—he would be giving *back* what they had originally already possessed. Similarly, and more realistically, a legislator might annul some galling statute or ordinance—an ordinance making it an offense to do business on the sabbath, for example, or to publish criticism of the established order. But in doing so he would not be *giving* anyone a freedom, except in the secondary sense already noted; for it was only as a consequence of human legislation that these freedoms, once possessed, were abridged in the first place. One should accordingly never think of civil liberties, for example, or of rights acknowledged in positive law, such as those guaranteed by the so-called Bill of Rights, as freedoms conferred by law. They are freedoms antedating law, having been (metaphorically) "conferred" by nature or (as some would prefer) by God. The law does not create them, but merely promises that no one will abridge them.

The continuum of freedom and bondage   Human freedom and human bondage are thus extreme opposites beyond which it is impossible to go in either direction. The one is *entirely* the creation of nature, and the other, the *entire* creation of men. More than this, whatever falls short of the one extreme, that of freedom, by however little, is the creation of men. Hardly anyone exemplifies either extreme—that is, few are in this day and age slaves, and few totally free from every conventional restraint. The lives of all of us coincide with some point on the continuum that reaches from one of these extremes to the other. If I am *totally* free, then my conduct is subject to a will, but it is no will but my own. I am in that case master of myself. If on the other hand I am in *total* bondage, then my conduct is again subject to a will, but it is a will that is *not* my own, and another man is my master. Few persons fit either description, though they to some extent fit both. Virtually all men are to *some* extent free; their conduct is to some extent subject to their own will. Similarly, all are to some extent in bondage; their conduct is to some extent involuntarily subject to the will of others. For example, I can rise and retire when I will, go, more or less, where I will, short of trespass, and so on; but I cannot take or use what I will, even though it may be at hand. The extent to which I am thus free defines, at the same time, the extent of my bondage; for that which I must do or refrain from doing, against my will, is precisely that respect in which I am not free, or am in bondage to the will of another.

The moral significance of freedom   Only a will that is free in the sense described—that is, not in subjugation to another—can be morally good. The will of a slave is neither morally good nor bad, for indeed such a will has for all practical purposes ceased to exist. God's will is of course thought of as holy, but this quality would be obliterated if the divine will were subject to some other alien will. And in the same sense only a free man can be morally estimable or, for that matter, morally reprehensible. Such freedom, or command over oneself and responsibility to oneself, is the precondition of a man's life that has any moral significance at all.

If we imagine a thief, for example, who steals entirely at the behest of another person who has him entirely within his power and can threaten him with severe injury for refusal to obey, then the opprobrium of the theft belongs not to the thief, but to his master. Conversely, if we imagine someone whose tireless energy is spent in good and noble works, but who is thereby serving merely as the puppet of another, then the praiseworthiness of that man's behavior instantly vanishes. His good works spring, not from his own will, but from fear and compulsion.

What, then, of obedience? Has this never any moral significance? Does the believer who says, "Not my will, but thine," thereby divest himself of moral responsibility for whatever he does in response to God's commands? And does the merit of the citizen decline in proportion to his loyalty to the state and obedience to its laws?

Fear vs. honor This question is slightly subtle, but important in throwing light on the underlying theme of the discussion.

Consider, then, first a man who obeys his ruler and the laws simply because he sees them as just and right, and who would perhaps decline to obey them, even at great peril to himself, if it were not for this justice and rightness. Such a man, if we consider the case carefully, has relinquished not the least bit of his freedom, for the will he responds to is still his own. He is still his own sovereign, for he bows, not to the *will* of any ruler, but to his *wisdom and goodness*. It is because the laws he is called upon to obey are just that he obeys them, and obeys from his own free will, and not because he is compelled to obey from fear, and without consideration of their justice.

If on the other hand we imagine a man who to the very same degree obeys his ruler and the laws, but does so from fear of the dreadful consequences of any failure to do so, then this is at once seen to be a man who is without freedom and without moral worth; for, since his obedience arises from fear, considerations of the justice and rightness of the commands that are laid upon him do not even arise. He would still obey, even if these commands or laws ceased to be right, for his fear would be unabated. He is accordingly not his own sovereign. He bows to the will of another and not to that other's wisdom and goodness; he obeys, not from his own free will, but from fear.

Thus the point stands that, except as one is sovereign to himself, his behavior is without moral significance. We see in these examples, however, how such freedom or sovereignty over oneself is at least compatible with a political life and with political obligation.

The same point can of course be made with respect to the believer. If, kneeling with bowed head, he declares, "Thy will be done," this does not necessarily represent the embodiment of virtue, though it may. It depends. If his head is bowed from fear of God's will and power, and from this alone, then he represents no virtue at all and might as well be a cowering animal. Had he the same fear of Satan, he would bow as readily and say to *him,* "Thy will be done." If on the other hand his head is bowed from reverence, the case is entirely otherwise; for this is totally compatible, not only with his freedom, but with his pride and humanity.

The problem of government   In the light of all the foregoing we can now formulate the fundamental problem of government in these terms.

A political society represents a relationship of rulers and ruled, or in other words, sovereignty and subjugation. In the modern state sovereignty is vested, not in one person, but in several. It ordinarily admits of degrees, but is rarely unlimited like a total despotism. It tends to be hierarchical, but this does not affect the basic relationship between sovereign and subject. That is, the citizen finds himself subject to the will of many persons, though in varying degrees, from the limited power of the local constabulary to the vast powers of a prime minister, president, legislature, politbureau, or party chairman. Each of these can, by threat, ordinarily but not necessarily expressed in statute or law, to some extent, great or small, bend the ordinary citizen to his own will.

The basic philosophical problem, then, is simply the justification of such an arrangement. Men are, as one likes to say, "born free." We have expressed this philosophically by saying that every man is by nature his own sovereign. The political state dilutes and compromises what every man thus has as a gift of nature. In some states this natural freedom is virtually abolished altogether. In others, typically in the democratic state, it is severely compromised. For it is of the very essence of government that those governed must obey, under threat of penalty for failure to do so. This is true of the modern democratic state as well as of the worst despotism. The alternative would be a state without laws and the machinery for enforcing them; and no such state exists, except on a minute scale, and would in fact not be a political state in the first place.

What, then, can justify anything so astonishing? The gravity of the philosophical problem can perhaps be seen by analogy with certain other qualities with which men are endowed by nature.

Men are, for example, more or less intelligent, by nature. This does not mean that they have no need to learn, by experience and otherwise, nor that human intelligence is ever unlimited; but the capacity to learn, and to reason and think, is natural to men. No man can ever point to any human contrivance or institution and say: I owe whatever intellectual capacities I possess to that. Human institutions can nourish intelligence or, conversely, stifle it, but they cannot create it. It is a gift of nature.

What, then, if certain men having the power to do so were *regularly* to stifle, mitigate, and ruin the natural intelligence of the vast majority of those within their power? Clearly, one could demand some justification for this, some end having sufficient value to warrant the payment of such a price.

Again, men possess the capacity for love and affection, and this is natural to them. This does not of course mean that all men are loving and affectionate, for it is a capacity that is easily and frequently corrupted. But human institutions do not create this capacity; they only, sometimes, cultivate it, as in the case of the institution of the family, or perhaps more commonly debase it, as in the case of such man-made things as the penitentiary, business corporation, and so on.

What, then, if some overwhelmingly powerful social institution made it its business to stifle and ruin whatever capacity for love and affection men have? Surely a reason or justification for this would be needed, and for the use of such a means, odious in itself; the purpose given would have to be one of overwhelming importance if it were to serve as a sufficient justification.

The case is no different for human freedom. We are born free, subject only to the determinations of our own wills, and only as such are we able to give our lives moral significance. Government, or the subjugation of the many by the few, represents a very severe dilution of that freedom; and this is so in the case of the best government as well as the worst. It is of the very nature of government that obedience to its laws is not entirely voluntary, but is enforced by the threat of punishment—that is, by fear. How, then, can this be justified? What end, if any, more precious than what is sacrificed for it, is thereby obtained?

Possible answers The philosophical imagination has been enormously fertile in supplying answers to this question, a few of which may be indicated here, if only to drive home the importance of the question. Some, for example, have thought that the ideal of a just state, as distinguished from a free one, serves as a justification. Others have argued that within the state a more perfect freedom is attained for its members, and that this ideal is obviously worth the sacrifice of personal freedom necessary to attain it. Still others have believed that there is in fact no such diminution of individual freedom in the state under certain conditions, viz., under the conditions of popular, freely chosen rulers. This is probably the most frequent justification and is often the rationale provided for the democratic society. A few thinkers, on the other hand, have argued eloquently that *nothing* can justify such a means, and that a condition of anarchism is the only morally justifiable arrangement that can be tolerated.

We shall address ourselves anew to this fundamental question, but not to this one alone, for although it underlies most other philosophical problems of government, it is not necessarily the most urgent one, or the most difficult.

The Philosophical Problems of Government

It is one thing to formulate the philosophical problems of government, but quite another to feel them as problems. So long as things are familiar and go along in accustomed ways, we feel little inclination to ask questions. It is only when we feel the pinch, when things pose threats to our interests, that intellectual justifications are apt to be sought. Thus a colony may suddenly "discover" that its king is without any clear authority to rule them when they find that he has imposed an onerous tax and that they have the means to resist his rule, whereas they had until then little reason for thinking of themselves as other than his subjects. Similarly, one cannot help being struck sometimes by the evident contentment of people living under the most corrupt despotism in which their basic needs appear to be met, though there seems to be not the slightest trace of legitimacy in the regime that has set itself over them, other than what can be conferred by the fear of guns in the hands of a loyal army.

It is, however, a mistake to suppose that philosophical problems of government exist only for citizens of nations other than one's own. We, no less than they, have from childhood been taught to deal with such problems in terms of slogans rather than of thought, so much so that it is common to find grown men, even men of intelligence and learning, solemnly intoning them. We are struck by the use of slogans in other cultures, particularly those headed by revolutionary regimes who look to certain writings and heroes for justification, but we easily overlook the extent to which slogans serve as substitutes for thinking on our own part.

Thus we are expected to say, for example, that in our system men are free to exercise their rights, provided they do not interfere with the rights of others; or again, that only under popular government, such as ours, are men truly free; or that democratic government is of, by, and for the people who are governed, and so on—epigrammatic summations of political philosophy that are not so much false as simply empty. They are in this respect rather like such claims as that a given dictatorship is the vanguard of the proletariat, that with the abolition of class conflict the state will wither away, etc., claims whose speciousness is far more evident to us than to those who have been taught to mouth them.

In the effort, then, to foster the state of mind in which it can be appreciated that there are philosophical problems of government, we propose a little fable. This story is slightly far-fetched in spots, but something of the sort seems desirable in order to penetrate the massive complacency that has been fortified in many by their indoctrination from childhood.

A little fable   Let us imagine a band of men—refugees or pilgrims, perhaps fleeing oppression—who have at last found a pleasant place to live in peace, a vast domain of rolling hills, fresh winding streams and green meadows, all conveying and supporting a natural sense of abundance and freedom, with ample space and means for their activities and pursuits. Here they raise their dwellings, sharing their domain over the years with their growing numbers of kinsmen, so that eventually everything has for them the feeling of familiarity and the kind of warmth and security men associate with being at home, in their own surroundings, with their own people.

Eventually, however, they begin to find men encamped here and there in what they had thought of as their homeland, men whose numbers greatly increase with time, until it becomes almost impossible to venture out without encountering them. They detect in them a patronizing attitude toward themselves and find that these men are all accompanied by, or can quickly summon, armed servants, ready at an instant to do their bidding. These servants keep a close eye on things, noting the comings and goings of the people and speculating on their purposes, from time to time peering into their windows to see what is going on there, noting down all their impressions, and regularly sending these along to someone they deferentially refer to as The Man. They also come around occasionally to help themselves to a certain fraction of the contents of everyone's pockets, according to a formula provided by The Man. Eventually it is discovered that high fences have gone up around the entire periphery of the place, intended, the people learn, to keep everyone inside. In case anyone should want to leave, to go through this high fence, he must first seek permission from The Man. Such permission, one is assured, will probably not be withheld, provided it is first established that the applicant has not violated any of a long and complex list of rules. These rules of course emanate from The Man—but not in any arbitrary or despotic way. Not at all. The people are themselves, they learn, the authors of them, at least for all practical purposes. Indeed, The Man and his servants make and enforce all these rules only with the prior consent of the people who must obey them. This is ensured in the most obvious and foolproof way imaginable, by their being given the opportunity every few years of writing The Man a letter—or at least, those who have obeyed all the rules are allowed to do this; the others are not. The letter is very succinct and to the point; so brief, in fact, that it contains only the single word "yes" or "no," which is meant to express how its author feels about The Man and his latest rules. In time this right of sending the letter, at quadrennial intervals, comes to be represented as the most precious blessing anyone can possess, far exceeding in its importance any interest he may have in anything else. It matters little what else one is allowed or forbidden to do as long as he is allowed to write this short letter every few years; for without this, he has *no* freedoms at all, whereas with this one, he has them *all*. At least, so everyone is told. No one actually looks at these letters, of course, except to pile them into two stacks and see which is higher; but they do serve the overwhelmingly important purpose of ensuring that the people who write them are free men, governed by their own consent, and of demonstrating that the often frivolous and sometimes galling rules enforced at every turn at the point of a gun do not really in any way delimit anyone's freedom at all. On the contrary, they guarantee for everyone a higher order of freedom. Nor are the rules really concocted by The Man, notwithstanding appearances, but by the people themselves, for that is what they were really doing, the last time they sent him their terse and friendly letters.

About half of the rules make sense. People are not supposed to go around hitting each other, for instance, nor taking each other's money without asking. The *Man* can take their money without asking, to be sure; in fact, once each year he sends agents around to reach into the peoples' pockets and take a fixed proportion of what they find there. If the agents meet with resistance, they end up taking whatever they want. But this is all right, since the people in effect told them they could do this by writing "yes" in their last letter. Or in the case of those who did not, then their neighbors did this for them. In any case, *someone* said "yes," which can accordingly be taken as the expression of each man's will.

So about half of the rules have some sense to them. The rest, however, are pulled out of a hat. People propose rules—any rules, it doesn't matter what they are—and these are all dropped into a hat and from time to time randomly drawn out. One of them is to the effect that no one may drink goat's milk except at certain hours and in certain precisely defined areas, and at exorbitant cost, most of the cost of it being a hidden tax that goes to The Man. Many people have an inordinate fondness for goat's milk, but some who tried it did not like it; so they put in the hat the rule that no one should ever have it at all, and that rule somehow got drawn from the hat. For awhile it was vigorously enforced, until modified by The Man in response to public clamor on the one hand and his desire for more revenue on the other. Another such rule, not so old and hence still uncompromisingly enforced, is that one may never drink tea, even at home, nor even possess it, even in molecular quantities. This rule was originally one of those drawn from the hat, of course, but it came to be represented as expressing the most basic of all those virtues that are traceable to the founding fathers and, some say, to God. Thus, in order to avoid public disgrace, a person has to sneak into a remote cave and there, in the darkness and isolation, proceed to brew it; if he is discovered, he is stripped, for the time being and perhaps for life, of the most basic human right to send a quadrennial letter to The Man, is made to turn over a considerable portion of his possessions, or else has obloquy heaped upon him and is locked up for years in one of the many zoos built for this purpose. Far worse than this, however, is selling tea—an act that is made the more hazardous by the fact that The Man pays his servants to be purchasers of it in order to trap people into selling it so he can send them off to the zoos.

There are many rules like that, drawn from the hat. In time some of them become obsolescent and are left unenforced, or are enforced only sporadically at the whim of The Man's armed servants; but others are always drawn from the hat to replace them. One of them, for example, requires that no adult male share his life with an adult female not related by blood without first obtaining The Man's permission and submitting to certain ritualistic procedures. Having once got this permission, gone through with the required forms, and begun such an arrangement, he may not then dissolve it without again soliciting permission from The Man, and this permission is given only with reluctance, if at all. One may not take two or more such persons under his roof under any circumstances whatever, at least not at the same time, The Man insisting on zealous enforcement of this rule always, having declared it to be essential to something or other.

The rules that are drawn from the hat are sometimes enforced with greater zeal than those in which one can discern some sort of point. Indeed, this is generally the case. For example, The Man long ago commissioned an artisan to carve out a huge wooden block that was oddly composed and resembled nothing in particular. This came to be referred to as "The Block," and eventually pictures of it began to appear everywhere. Songs were written about The Block, verses composed; these are now intoned with an air of solemnity wherever people foregather. Children are taught, upon arriving at school, to put small replicas of The Block on their heads and hop about on one foot for a minute or two while reciting verses about The Block and affirming their devotion to it. Lifelong habits are thus created. For instance, even old men, upon hearing Block refrains, leap to their feet as a reflex and hop about, clapping both hands on their heads (after first removing their hats); and scornful glances are directed to anyone who may be slow in doing this.

Periodically everyone takes a day off from work to honor The Man and his servants, particularly those trained in the use of knives, guns, and grenades. At these times replicas of The Block are seen everywhere: people set them out on their porches and yards, in their windows, on their roofs, and on their cars. Exhortations are struck and displayed for the general edification, always in juxtaposition to replicas of The Block. The simplest and commonest is: "Honor your Block." One of the more inspirational is: "Ask not what The Man can do for you; rather ask, what you can do for The Man." Although apparently no one ever does actually ask such a question, and would be suspected of having been drinking goat's milk if he did, such sentiments and the evocation of feelings that are everywhere associated with The Block are thought to render people less bilious when The Man's emmisaries come around to rifle through their pockets and help themselves to what they find there, or to peer in their windows to see what might be going on, or to break into rooms to see whether they can find any tea.

The problems of government   One could hardly maintain that this yarn bears no resemblance to the lot of any people with whom we are familiar. Perhaps then, it can serve as the background for the philosophical problems enunciated before, problems that must be dealt with, not fabulously, but philosophically. The people just described could certainly, with great justification, ask (1) What is the rational justification for the government of some men by others, in case any exists? Do we obey because we are slaves and have to, from fear of threats, or is government justified in what it demands of us? Further, they could with great justice ask (2) What renders the rule of this government legitimate, in preference to rule by others who might, for example, fulfill our needs better? Again, they could properly ask (3) What, after all, is the purpose of government—to perpetuate allegiance to its own trappings? To ensure us greater security? To enable us to pursue our own happiness? Or what? Similarly, the more thoughtful among them would insist upon asking (4) What is the proper extent of governmental authority and control over the individual? Where do our liberties end, and the coercive power of government begin? And finally, it is clearly important for them to wonder (5) What are our duties as citizens? To obey all the laws? Or only those that are just? Do our obligations as men transcend our duties as citizens of this commonwealth? Or is it the other way around?

It will of course be noted that these are precisely the five questions listed at the outset. For the intelligent people in the fable, they would be, not just abstract questions of philosophy, but questions of the most overwhelming importance that reach to the very basis of human happiness and the rationale of social and political life. And so they are for us, for our lot is not so different from that of those fabulous citizens, and our problems are essentially the same. It may be that all these questions have answers that do not in the least threaten the established order under which we live. On the other hand, the answers to them may leave that order with no support whatever that human reason can accept. Or the truth may, of course, lie somewhere between these extremes.

The Significance of Rules IV

It is worth reminding ourselves of something obvious—namely, that just as government, law, and morality were not imparted to the world at its creation, neither were the philosophical problems they have engendered. All laws and governments are the creation of men themselves, and so are the philosophical problems.

No reminder of this elementary point would in the least be needed, were it not for the tendency of thinkers to rest their intellectual creations upon certain philosophical principles as though these were eternal things, and then step back in astonishment to discover, from time to time, that those principles have led them into paradox. This is especially the case in philosophical politics and ethics. It is fairly common for political philosophers just to presuppose the notion of *human rights,* for example, taking for granted that there simply *are* such things, and even offering to list a few of the more basic ones. When they find that certain practices and institutions of human creation tend to compromise those alleged rights, they conclude that those practices and institutions have thereby been cast in a dubious light and perhaps should be jettisoned—it never occurring to them that human rights are themselves human creations. Or again—and this is something even more pernicious—it is simply taken for granted that there are such things as moral duty, moral responsibility, and moral law, quite apart from the derivations of conventional political and religious systems. When they discover that certain political institutions, or even the institution of government itself, compromises what is presupposed as some necessary condition of moral responsibility, then again, they cast doubt upon those institutions. We have even lately been treated to an eloquent treatise in defense of *anarchy* on precisely this basis—i.e., that *all* government is inconsistent with something that is blithely presupposed as a precondition of an antecedently existing moral responsibility.* While no one doubts that government, or at least this or that form of it, is of human invention, it somehow does not occur to these speculative thinkers to wonder whether the same might be true of their notions of morality. The fact that certain abstract moral principles have been roundly and eloquently set forth by philosophers of old, and sometimes declared to be the fruit of an *a priori* practical reason, does not show that they are not the product of certain very human attempts to deal with the threats of an empirical world. It only demonstrates that, as philosophers with a natural predilection for eternal things, they do not like to so think of them. But after all, as the Declaration of Independence suggests, as well as the dogmatics of some contemporary thinkers, it is just as possible to think of certain governmental forms in the same absolute terms—a poor way to go about resolving the problems of government.

The idea of a state of nature   Some classical philosophers tried to get down to basics and rid their minds of the prejudices of their age by considering that "state of nature" which they thought antedated the establishment of government. They then speculated upon the manner in which men emerged from that primitive condition, in order to see more clearly how government might have come about, what its justification was, and what form of government was proper in the light of such speculative history. Of course they were not really able to divest themselves of certain ideas that could only have been the product of civilized, or governed, life. They generally imagined such natural prehistoric men as coming together and working things out more or less philosophically, for example, then entering into formal contracts, setting up kingships, and so on.

But the basic idea was a good one; that is, the idea of making a beginning on these problems by stripping away some of the philosophical and conceptual accretions that may be the sources of problems. If we want to resolve the philosophical problems of government, a promising approach is to try to see how and why, in general, a legal order arises in the first place. And having made that start, we should go back one more step, not usually taken, and see how the ideas of right and wrong arise, as well as others of significance to political philosophy, such as good and bad, obligation, human rights, and so on.

* See Chapter VIII.

In doing this we need not imagine that we are reconstructing history. We are simply exercising our imaginations wherein certain states of affairs involving men rather like ourselves exist, and then bringing the implications out. In *imagining* a body of men without government, for example, and then asking what would be the likely consequences of such life, we need not say when, or even whether, such a body of men has existed. That might be an interesting anthropological study, but it is of no particular philosophical relevance.

Let us start at rock bottom, then, and imagine a solitary man, bound by no constraints other than those he imposes on himself, and note the extent and the limitation of his freedom, his innocence, and his misery.

A man who had the world entirely to himself would be absolutely *free* and totally *innocent*. This does not mean that he would have a good life, and in fact it takes little reflection to see that his life would be abysmally awful; but he would nevertheless have these two precious ingredients of a blissful existence that none of us entirely possesses.

Let us see why this is so, and see how, without giving up too much of what we have, we might improve upon our limited share of these two blessings that our solitary man has in such abundance.

Right and wrong   A man alone in the world could not possibly commit any wrong. His actions might be skillful or clumsy, sagacious or foolish, beneficial or injurious to himself; but they could not be morally right or morally wrong. These ideas just do not apply here. Such a man might wisely and prudently provide for his own future by storing food or preparing against impending cold; but such actions could hardly be right, morally estimable, noble, or just. They could only be prudent. Similarly, he might foolishly or carelessly or, perhaps, deliberately injure himself by failing to make such provision against a threatening future or by wounding himself; but such actions could hardly be morally wrong, blameworthy, ignoble, or unjust. They could only be careless, clumsy, or imprudent. A man who benefits or injures no one but himself is not accountable for his actions, nor deserving either of praise or blame. He is incapable of any wickedness and equally incapable of moral heroism or even of the simplest moral virtue. He is, precisely, innocent of both.

Suppose such a man foolishly neglected to provide for his own future, running the risk of starvation or cold, perhaps with the full knowledge of such risk, just to enjoy some ephemeral pleasure, or even from sheer laziness. Would this not be wrong?

No, it would be foolish. In ascribing wrongness we are importing a new idea altogether that nothing in the circumstances suggests—unless, of course, one is merely using this strong term of condemnation to call attention to that man's folly and to condemn it.

Or suppose he were to curse God, or worship false gods, or deliberately and willfully violate certain other of God's commands, as Adam and Eve are charmingly thought to have done. Would this not be wrong? Perhaps—assuming that there is a God who has commanded this man, and who is for some reason entitled to obedience. But now note what has happened. We are no longer thinking of this man as being strictly alone in the world. We have added no fellow men to this company, to be sure, but we have introduced another person, God himself, considered as a being capable of enunciating commands and expecting obedience. The point still stands, then, that a *truly* solitary being, though capable of folly, would be incapable of either moral virtue or wickedness. He would be totally innocent of both.

Right and wrong in relation to rules   But this innocence, we must now note, is not solely because of his solitude. If the man we are imagining shares the world with someone else, or with several, and interacts with others in numerous ways so that what he does affects their weal and woe, then his actions do not, solely by virtue of this, suddenly become invested with the qualities of moral right and wrong. If, for example, we imagine our man eating, then this action, considered by itself, obviously has no quality of moral rightness or wrongness. Nor does it acquire either quality when we add the further supposition that the animal he is eating was felled by another, or that the fruit he is eating was planted by someone else. We might feel tempted at first to say that, in this case, he has committed a theft—but that is only because *we* have defined theft and declared it to be a wrong, and are now applying this idea where it has not been defined or associated with any moral response. The idea of theft is without meaning apart from the idea of *property;* and the idea of property, as distinct from possession, is the creation of men. To *possess* something is merely to hold it or have it within one's power, and what one thus holds he may forcibly lose to another, whose possession it becomes from that moment. But one may *own* what he does not yet possess, and may still own it after being forcibly dispossessed of it—simply because the idea of ownership or property is a conventional one, the creation of men. And with the emergence of the idea of property there arises also the idea of theft, which had no meaning before.

Therefore, right and wrong are relative to and in fact wholly derivative from commands or, more often, customary practices or rules, which are in turn the creations of men. The distinction of moral right and wrong does not exist antecedently, as part of some metaphysical or ethical framework of the universe that is merely awaiting discovery by men through the exercise of practical reason or otherwise, nor awaiting revelation by God through his prophets. This is why the distinction has no application in the world of a hermit. The reason is not merely that there is no one in that world for the hermit to *injure,* but because nothing is *forbidden.* The ideas of right and wrong are inseparable from those of permission and prohibition, and these are in turn inseparable from rules or commands.

What a rule is   A rule need not, of course, be anything very formal, like a statute or an item of the Decalogue, nor need it even be anything promulgated by any authority, such as a king or legislator, nor even enunciated or in any way reduced to words. It need be no more than a custom —that is, a regular (Lat. *regula*) mode of behavior more or less expected and predictable. Given a rule, then, in at least this minimal sense, an action will be *wrong* in case it is a breach of that rule; otherwise, it will be innocent (permitted). Eliminate the idea of a rule, thus broadly conceived, and you thereby eliminate also every distinction between right and wrong.

   With respect to the solitary man for example, we raised the question whether it might not be *wrong* of him to curse God or violate the divine commands, and the point was made that we were no longer imagining a truly *solitary* man. Note what has happened, however, with the introduction of the idea of a command—in this case, a command from God. The distinction of right and wrong has suddenly appeared, ushered in with the notion of a command, where before there was not the least trace of such an idea. It was not, in other words, the mere fact that we were importing into the picture another person—in this case, God—and thus rendering our solitary man no longer solitary. The mere *presence* of such an additional being, even one who is almighty, can no more give birth to the distinction between right and wrong than can the presence of the sun and the moon. It is, rather, the presence of this being *as possessing a will,* and making that will known through the expression of commandments or rules, which creates this distinction.

An ancient problem of ethics   Of course the suggestion is bound to arise at this point that the author of such commands is, after all, God Almighty, and that we are therefore doing considerably more than merely introducing a being with a will. God, it will be thought, has not only a will that is made known, but goodness as well, and these commandments are a reflection of God's goodness rather than of a blind and omnipotent will. God, in other words, is imagined as a being having the *right* or the *authority* to command and not just the *power* to enforce obedience. He must, therefore, command what he does *because it is right;* it does not become right simply as a consequence of His commanding it.

   It would seem, therefore, that the distinction between right and wrong is *not* merely relative to rules. On the contrary, the rules, if they are to deserve our respect and compliance, must be *right*—something that would be automatically assured if they issued from a divine will.

This point is as old as the philosophy of Socrates (see Plato's *Euthyphro*) and perpetually arises to muddle men's minds. We shall return to it shortly, but for now let us revert in imagination to our very simple "society," that is, not to our hermit, but to the multiplicity of men living in proximity to each other, but without any government (tribal chieftain or whatnot) and, let us suppose, without any religion whatever. Even so, we can presume that they tend to behave in accordance with at least a few very basic rules necessary for having any kind of common life, without at all bringing in God to give them rules, or a legislator to enact them, or a committee that assembled and agreed upon them, or anything of the kind. We can suppose, for example, that the custom has gradually arisen that, say, any animal killed shall "belong" to him who felled it, that his *possession* (grasping) of it is not to be challenged. Similarly, any fruit shall be his who first found it, or who grew it. And similarly, any object whatever shall be his who first picked it up, and any parcel of land his who first staked its boundaries and took to living upon it.

Now, *why* would such men ever come to live in accordance with such customs and rules? We may imagine that a forceful leader has told them to. Or we may imagine that a Moses has told them to and convinced them that the gods they fear expect them to. We might even (though this is far-fetched) emulate the philosophers of an earlier period and imagine that these men themselves have assembled, reasoned together, and then entered into a *covenant* or *contract* to behave in these ways toward each other. But of course we do not need to import any of those more or less sophisticated notions at all. We can instead suppose that over the course of time they have found it to their *mutual advantage* to behave in these ways, that such behavior thus becomes customary, more or less habitual, and above all, therefore *expected*. Given such customs, or modes of behavior that are generally adhered to and thus expected, it becomes "wrong" to act contrary to them; and the idea of *theft,* for example, which had no existence before, now emerges as meaningful. It is not at all unlikely, of course, that in such a simple society, and in response to perfectly obvious human needs, the attempt will be made to regulate behavior in ways more secure than mere reliance upon custom—that, for example, someone will arise to give such customs the force of divine commands, as Moses did, or the force of law, as governments do, or the association with justice, as philosophers and jurisconsults have done. But these things, and in particular the idea of justice, are neither rationally nor temporally *prior* to, and thus neither validate nor give rise to the distinction between right and wrong. Right and wrong, and hence justice, must be understood in terms of convention and practice, which are the creations of men, rather than the other way around.

In the manner, then, in which the idea of theft arises, so also do other wrongs come into being—bigamy, adultery, trespass, breach of contract, perjury, poaching, murder, and so on down the list. One does not poach simply by shooting a wild animal, for example, but by doing so at a forbidden time and place, or in other words, in violation of convention or rule. Similarly, adultery is carnal knowledge of a married person—but what counts as "married" is the creation of custom and rule. Or again, with respect to an example in which the error being illustrated is often committed, one does not commit murder merely by willfully taking the life of another human being. One can *kill* a man in the absence of a rule, but not *murder* him in such absence of rule. In the light of this one can see the absurdity of such familiar remarks as "abortion (or war, or drunken driving) is murder." They are not, unless and until so defined by rule, whether the rule be made by man or, as some would prefer, made by God. When Moses (speaking, it is said, on behalf of Yahweh) said "Thou shalt not kill," this was interpreted to mean that it was forbidden to kill *other men*. It could without absurdity have been understood to mean that one was not to kill other men *nor their livestock,* in which case it would have been perfectly possible to murder a goat. But as things stand—i.e., given the rule as it has in fact been interpreted—it is not possible to murder a goat. One can only slaughter it. Men have, from certain practical considerations not very difficult to fathom, preferred to reserve the opprobrium of murder for the doing of death to their own kind. Swift's Houyhnhnms would have found it more in keeping with the precepts of practical reason to have it the other way about.

The practical basis of rules   What, then, of the age-old question posed by Socrates and still considered to be so terribly penetrating: Does God love certain things because they are holy, or are they holy simply because loved by God? Or in our terms: Are certain things forbidden because they are wrong, or are they wrong simply because they are forbidden?

The difficulty with such a question is not that it is so deep and philosophical but simply that it is ineptly expressed. It is put in such a way as to allow only two choices of answer when the truth quite plainly lies in another direction altogether. The correct answer can be expressed as follows: In the course of time men find it to their mutual advantage to behave in certain ways which, because such behavior is useful, become more or less customary and habitual. As these customs and habitual modes of behavior become settled, the departure from them comes to be met with resentment, with feelings that assume the form of moral disapproval, censure, or blame. In order to secure more reliable adherence to these behavior patterns, which is not sufficiently guaranteed by mere custom and habit, they often come to be explicitly enjoined by positive rules. These rules are then given added force by being represented as coming from God and transmitted by his prophets or, failing that, from some antecedently existing principles of morals and transmitted by an *a priori* practical reason. At *that* point philosophical minds raise the question whether the rules ought to be respected because what they command is morally right, or whether such rightness is simply the consequence of there being such rules, the absurdity of the second choice forcing one, they think, to adopt the first. One should have said, however, that the behavior enjoined by the rules is to be adopted because it is to the mutual advantage of those living under the rules, that because of this advantage it is desirable to make such behavior a matter of explicit positive rule, and that in the light of such rule, but only in that light, it is possible to speak of moral right and wrong. From all of which it follows that, if and when there *ceases* to be any practical point to the behavior in question, then there likewise ceases to be any justification for behaving that way. It would be a *total* misunderstanding to say that such behavior is, after all, enjoined by the moral law, or by God, or by practical reason, or whatnot, and must, therefore, be right. Even philosophers, however addicted to abstractions, are not entitled to disregard the question of where such ideas are derived from.

Good and Evil V

We have spoken thus far of right and wrong, which is a distinction that applies only to actions. We have said nothing of good and evil, which is a much more comprehensive pair of opposites, applicable not only to human actions but to anything under the sun. Thus things as diverse as rain, sun, food, pain, shelter, warmth, love, bacteria, and hurricanes can all under certain circumstances be described as being good or as being bad; but it makes no sense to speak of any of those things as right or wrong. Shelter, for example, is neither right or wrong, though it is under most circumstances good. The *provision* of shelter for one's children, on the other hand, is normally right—but there we are again speaking of action—the act of providing something.

Good and evil as distinctions of the will   While rights and wrongs are, as indicated, the creations of customs and conventions and thus relative to rules, it is clear that good and evil are not so in the least, but are instead relative only to the nature of those beings, such as men, by whom they are felt.

Thus the solitary man with whom we began, for whom the distinction of right and wrong had no meaning, nevertheless distinguishes between good and bad. This is essentially the distinction between things sought and things shunned; and no rules, customs, or conventions, nor even the society of one's fellows, are in any way needed for this. We need only to suppose that such a being has certain needs, desires, or aims, that he is by his various actions trying to accomplish various things, in order to see exactly what things seem to him good, and what things bad. *Good* are those things he finds that satisfy his needs, desires, and aims; and *bad* those that frustrate these.

There is, of course, an epistemological factor here, in that one might be mistaken in what he takes to promise fulfillment of his needs. Thus one might think that something before him (for example, water) offers satisfaction of some need (thirst), when in fact it threatens the very opposite (being contaminated by poison). This combination of a desiderative and an epistemic or rational factor raises some nice problems of rational choice that Socrates and others never tired of dwelling on, and we shall return to them shortly. For now, however, the point remains that good and evil for a given being are relative to that being's needs, aims, and desires.

Consider a man alone in the world, for example, with only a few basic desires. We can suppose that the most fundamental and persistent of these is the desire to stay alive, and along with this the desires to be free from hunger, cold, and danger. Now it is clear that what this man perceives as making his life more secure he will also perceive as good, and for no other reason than that it does appear to him as promising security. Similarly, what he perceives as food, warmth, and safety he will also perceive as good, just because these will satisfy his felt needs. Moreover, in case he is in fact right in believing that something—some shelter, for example—will enhance his security, then he cannot possibly be wrong in regarding it as good. Similarly, if he is right in believing that something— some fruit he has found, for example—will remove his felt hunger without presenting new threats and dangers, then again, he cannot be wrong in thinking of it as good. Thus, in short, the distinction between good and evil will be to this man precisely the distinction between those things that will assist him, and those that will hinder; those that will satisfy, and those that will frustrate; or roughly, those that hold promise, and those that hold threat. Good and evil are thus relative to one's desires or goals, and have no existence apart from these. No rules, customs, or conventions are needed for the existence of desires or goals, however, nor do we need to presuppose any multiplicity of desiderative beings. One is enough, for as soon as we postulate just one being who has desires, needs, and goals, and lives in some sort of environment that offers promise and threat to the satisfaction of these, then the distinction between good and evil emerges, and it emerges as *complete*.

The role of reason   Complete, yes—but not such as to render choice *infallible*. It is the confusion of these two ideas that has led many moralists and political philosophers, beginning with Socrates and Plato, into some strange conceptions of justice and government. Obsessed with the role that knowledge and reason must play in the choice of good and the avoidance of evil, they actually *equated* justice with knowledge; and most moralists since have had no doubt that reason is essential even to drawing the distinction between them. It is not at all. The distinction itself is made by the will, by the desiderative side of our nature—the very thing that most moralists, from Socrates and St. Paul to Kant, have wanted to push into the background, wishing, one would think, that it didn't even exist. Reason and knowledge, on the other hand, enter in only as guides to the choice of means for attaining the good and avoiding the bad.

Consider, for example, the situation adumbrated a moment ago. Let us suppose one is parched with deep, demanding, unremitting thirst, and in this condition suddenly finds himself before a fountain of clear, cool, sweet water. Plainly, it would appear good to him. Could he be mistaken?

The answer is both yes and no, or rather, part is yes, and part no. The basic distinction between good and evil that is expressed in this situation is not that one could be wrong. There is the state of need or desire (thirst), the perception of something which, *it is rightly or wrongly believed,* would satisfy that need, and the consequent response of the will. There is at this point no judgment, and hence, neither error nor truth. Thus is the distinction between goodness and badness made to begin with, and *it* is not the sort of thing that is subject to correction. If the fountain were not one of clear fresh water but something else—of black and foul-smelling sewage and slime, let us suppose—then the response of the will would be very different; and again, this would not be the sort of thing that would be subject to correction. All that has emerged, at this point of the analysis, is the distinction between good and evil; and the point that must really be fixed for good, not to be subsequently dislodged by subtle dialectic, is that this distinction is (in this example) wholly relative to the needs and desires of the being who makes it. It could not even exist, were it not for those needs and desires.

Where, then, does fallibility begin? If the distinction between good and evil is one that exists only in relation to the will and is not drawn by reason, how can one possibly be mistaken in his choice of good or his aversion to evil?

The answer to this is already quite plainly before us, for reason does enter in here, in the judgment of what the situation actually is. It is a judgment of means to end, which can be a mistaken one. Thus even a fountain of clear, fresh, sweet water might have been poisoned by his enemies, so that, while he is not "wrong" in desiring to quench his deep thirst, and to do so by what he takes to be at hand, he *is* wrong in thinking that this is the way to do it. What he wants is to drink, not to be poisoned. The error has solely to do with the means to an end. The end itself cannot be wrong nor, for that matter, can it be right—except, perhaps, in relation to still further ends.

Good and evil as distinctions of nature   We thus see how the distinction between right and wrong arises among beings who, like ourselves, join in a common or political life, at whatever level, and how the quite different distinction between good and evil arises. The first is generated by rules, minimally conceived, and the second by our desiderative or conative nature, by the fact that we have needs and desires, or better, by the fact that we are goal-seeking beings. This latter distinction, between good and evil, is plainly the more basic one, for it is only in relation to the fulfillment of our ends and purposes that there is any point to having rules, customs, or conventions in the first place. A race of beings who had no interest in anything, a race of beings who were, like machines, without will would have no need for rules governing the manner in which their aims might be pursued, for they would be without any aims. Distinctions of right and wrong would thus have no application to them precisely because, in the last analysis, the distinction of good and evil would be inapplicable too.

Furthermore—and this is a point that can have enormous consequences—the distinction between good and evil is a distinction of *nature* and not, like right and wrong, merely one of *convention*. Men create their customs, conventions, and rules, and everything that is brought into the service of these, such as government; but they do not create the prior distinction between good and evil, for they do not create themselves, nor their wills, nor their ultimate ends and aims, which are the product of their wills. These are bestowed (or inflicted) on them as part of their nature, neither to glorify nor to repudiate, but simply to fulfill. The fulfillment of them is happiness, or simply, human goodness or beatitude; and the frustration of them wretchedness, or simply, human evil or misery. Those formulae probably contain the answers to virtually every problem that has ever been raised in philosophical ethics, but they answer none of the philosophical problems of government. Instead, they *pose* all those problems, the most basic one being: How, through government, or perhaps through the abolishment of government, is such goodness to be attained and misery overcome?

Freedom and the Highest Good   VI

The philosophical as distinct from the practical problems of government arise from two related and simple facts about men: namely, first, that they are possessed of both reason and will, and second, that these wills almost inevitably conflict as soon as any kind of social life is entered into, even though that society may have only two members. The will gives meaning to the concept of happiness; and reason seeks, wisely or ineptly, to comprehend it and discover the means to it.

The possibilities of error are accordingly threefold. First, they are *rational,* resulting in the unfit choice of the means to happiness—for example, bad procedures, bad institutions, or bad government; second, they are *conceptual,* arising from an imperfect conception of the end, which is happiness, erroneously identifying it with power, possession, and similar errors; and third, they are *moral,* involving the wrong resolution of the conflict of aims, as in the case of exploitation or the generation of poverty.

Happiness and the will   Men are not machines, devoid of desire. If they were, there would be no problem of government, for there would be no need of government. Nothing whatever would matter. Nor are men like houseflies or foxes, assembling from time to time into purely accidental associations or for transient purposes such as reproduction. A fox remains a fox, though a solitary one, but a solitary man does not for long remain a man, except in the minimal sense that he retains the marks of that animal species. Nor finally, are men like the social insects, whose individual wills and aims have become so totally submerged as to have almost disappeared altogether. No conflict of aims can arise in such a society because there are no individual aims that can present such a possibility. In the case of men, however, only two are needed to create the possibility and in fact the almost inevitable threat of conflict of aims—a conflict that can be resolved only by gross physical means (war and subjugation), or by rules, i.e., by a system of law and government.

The conflict of aim   If, reverting to our previous experiments of imagination, we now go one more step and postulate a multiplicity of men living in proximity to each other such that what one of them does can affect the weal and woe of the others, then we produce no *new* distinction between good and evil, though we greatly enlarge the possibilities for their emergence. The distinction itself was originally one between those things that assist and those that hinder the fulfillment of aim, and so it remains. The complication that is introduced by postulating a multiplicity of desiderative beings is that their aims *conflict* and thereby create the possibility of war or, conversely but less probably, *coalesce* toward a common end and thereby create the possibility of cooperation. It is upon those simple facts that social and political philosophy finally rest.

Imagine, for example, a multiplicity of men, all hungry, in the presence of food sufficient to satisfy only one of them. It is inevitable that the satisfaction of the need of one must necessarily result in the frustration of the needs of all the rest, and that good will therefore be inseparable from evil. It is precisely this kind of situation that gives rise to the need for rules, of which we have already spoken. If men's needs were so modest that there was never the threat to anyone that his needs might be unfulfilled, or if the resources of the environment were so vast that the frustration of any need would never appear as a real possibility, then probably no rules would ever be needed for a common life, and hence, no distinction of right and wrong would ever arise or occur to anyone. All men, under such benign conditions, would be as innocent, and as free, as that solitary one with whom we began. Nothing would incline them to injure, and hence no rule would be needed to restrain them. Living outside the constraint of any rules, these men would be utterly free.

The absolute good   If the fulfillment of aim, purpose, or desire is good, and the frustration of these bad, then the greatest or absolute good of any man can be nothing less than complete fulfillment. This is the *summum bonum* of the philosophers, the *eudaimonia* of the Greeks, or simply, human happiness. A corollary of this is that the greatest good for a society of persons is the fulfillment of ends of each and all of its members and,

even more grandly, that the greatest good for mankind is the total fulfillment of every human end and the elimination of want.

As they stand these formulas are altogether too broad and sweeping
to be very valuable, and of course they present enormous possibilities for
misunderstanding. Indeed, it would hardly be an exaggeration to say that
most rationalistic moral and political philosophy, beginning with Plato,
has arisen from a misrepresentation of what is involved in these concepts,
and in particular from misrepresenting the connection between human
reason and will in the search for happiness.

We cannot here undertake a disquisition on the nature of human
happiness because the subject is too large and belongs to moral rather than
political philosophy, but some clarification is necessary in order to avoid
fatal misunderstandings.

Ignorance of the means to happiness   First, then, it was said that, a man's
good being the satisfaction of a need, his absolute good must be total
fulfillment of his needs. This does not mean the fulfillment of his *felt*
needs, which can of course be capricious, uninformed, or in conflict with
each other; nor is it the fulfillment of what he *believes* are his needs, since
such beliefs, like any others, can be mistaken. Thus, a man can, in the
manner illustrated a moment ago, be quite mistaken in his choice of means
to an end: he can seek to satisfy his thirst with water that is poisoned, for
example, or seek salvation by embracing the creed of a religion not known
to be false, and thus court damnation; or, to cite one of Plato's favorite
examples, seek well-being through power, greed, and self-aggrandizement,
and through those ill-chosen means be rewarded with wretchedness.

Ignorance of the end   But there is another possibility for error slightly
more subtle and insidious, and that is error concerning the end itself. That
is, one can be wrong in believing that some goal of his is worth pursuing,
precisely because the fulfillment of *that* goal is not ultimately satisfying.
This is, in fact, the general description of the wasted life. It is a life spent
in the pursuit of specious goals, goals that were for one reason or another
alluring and seemed to promise fulfillment, but were then found to be
worthless in their attainment. Plato's wretched tyrant can be viewed in
this light, too—that is, he mistook a certain means (power) as an end in
itself (well-being) and then was made wretched by lack of fulfillment, even
though *his* end was attained. Examples more familiar come readily to the
mind of anyone who has observed the world around him reflectively, for
the wasted life is a baneful commonplace of that world, and it consists
simply of this—stupidity in the choice of the sort of end that can give
human existence meaning.

Philosophers have tended to suppose that, the possibility of error here being so overwhelming, and the need of wisdom so correspondingly compelling, good and evil must themselves be understood in terms of reason rather than desire. The fact does remain, however, that if men were beings without will, if men had *no* aims or desires, then nothing at all would be good and nothing bad, and we would resemble statues and stones more than living striving men, quite regardless of any rational endowments. Good and evil are therefore relative to the will, are in fact its product, and can be defined only in terms of fulfillment. In no other way can meaning be given to the notion of happiness, which must otherwise be only the name of an abstraction—which, incidentally, it has largely become at the hands of more than a few philosophers.

Happiness and wisdom   Happiness might then be defined as the fulfillment of enlightened desire, thus taking account both of the familiar fact that impulsive behavior, even when it leads to the satisfaction of impulse, can land one in wretchedness, and of the equally indubitable fact that enlightenment or understanding by itself is sterile. There is nothing gained by illuminating a pathway if one has no desire to walk that path, and ends or purposes, which are the ends or purposes of no one, are simply nonentities to which a name has been given. Every man with a will, and thus every genuinely human being, seeks fulfillment, for that is what it means to be a volitional being; but every man of reason and thus again, every genuinely human being seeks real and lasting fulfillment and well-being through enlightened and intelligent choice. Human misery is sometimes the product of circumstances, as we see in cases of famines and wars, but it is also sometimes the product of one's own folly. In such cases satisfaction was sought *and won,* but stupidly. In this picture we see the profound truth of the Socratic claim that "virtue" or goodness is not attainable without wisdom.

Happiness and the common good   Human happiness should not be identified with the common good; the former is an ideal of personal ethics and the latter a guiding consideration of the formulation of public policy. Thus government should aim at protecting the common good, but not necessarily at the happiness of those governed—paternalism is not an appropriate role of the state. The common good is better thought of as being opposed to privilege, which is the fulfillment of individual aim *at the expense* of the rest when it would have been possible to seek the good of all. Thus, for example, if the private ownership of land is extended to the private ownership of areas used exclusively for recreation, such as seashores and parks, enabling a few persons to enjoy unlimited use of these and depriving the rest of any use of them at all, then consideration of the public good has been disregarded. Such policies could be described in terms of human happiness, but it is not necessary, and it is likely to be vague or misleading. Furthermore, it is in keeping with the purpose of government to seek the common good, but not to seek happiness. Law protects only the pursuit of happiness; it does not guarantee its attainment.

The conditions of absolute good   The fulfillment that is happiness, therefore, is the fulfillment of our needs and purposes as men, and not merely the fulfillment of such needs as happen to be felt by this man or that. Error is possible, both in how to attain what we want and in what we want, and wretchedness is the reward of the one as well as the other. Just *what* is the final end of man, or that which really and not just seemingly promises fulfillment (which is human well-being or happiness), is the ultimate question of moral philosophy. Here we only assert that there is such a thing, and when the fulfillment of needs and desires is spoken of as good, this is always to be understood as qualified in both ways described; namely, the fulfillment of genuine and not specious or illusory needs, and the choice of means that are effective and do not merely seem so.

Absolute good has been described in terms of fulfillment, as that which really does satisfy and put to rest struggle and striving, rather than merely offering some promise of doing so. Such unqualified happiness, although serving as an appropriate ideal of personal ethics, is not a realistic objective of social and political philosophy, for compromise and restraint are part of the very mechanism of political life, as we shall abundantly see. Living together, we seek first of all security and rightly consider ourselves blessed if our *pursuit* of happiness, which is all we are guaranteed, does in some measure succeed.

For now we need only note that there appear to be but two ways in which any man could find that total fulfillment which would be his absolute good; first, in case his needs were exceedingly meager and thus easily surfeited, and second, in case his environment were so benign and his fellow men so loving that he would be assured complete fulfillment, no matter how vast and compelling his needs might be.

Imagine, if possible, a man who has but a single desire, that one being simply the desire to continue in existence for a finite time—say, another month. We suppose him to be devoid of any other interest or aim, having only this incredibly paltry one. He does not care whether he is warm or cold, hungry or filled, cares nothing about what surrounds him. As long as he exists for an additional month, he will be entirely satisfied; he requires absolutely nothing more. In the case of such a man (if a being so pruned and truncated can be thought of as a man), the satisfaction of this one trivial desire will be his absolute good. Its goodness cannot be enhanced by the addition of any further satisfactions, there being no further desires to be satisfied. And clearly *this* absolute or final good, his good, might be quite attainable, it being no feat merely to exist for a while.

Actual men are not, however, of such contemptible constitution as to be, like some sort of bacterium, satisfied with so little; and so the *summum bonum* of men as we actually find them is not so easily guaranteed.

Imagine on the other hand, then, men more like ourselves but dwelling in a paradise. What defines their abode as a paradise is that it presents no possibility whatever of pain or frustration to any man, but on the contrary promises complete fulfillment, both because it is bountiful and because it is loving, so that there is neither the need nor the incentive to the least competition. Under these conditions, again, the absolute good might be quite attainable.

Our actual world, however, is not like this, but on the contrary presents on every side the threat of wretchedness, such that the mere escape from this, to enjoy a bit of rest, consumes the greater part of our energy; and in their competition for this uncertain security and for such fulfillment as can be won, our fellow men are far from loving and are considered to have risen fairly high in the direction of an ideal humanity if they so much as succeed in mutual restraint. The attainment of the *summum bonum* in the world as we actually find it, therefore, is not a possible goal for mankind as a whole.

The greatest possible good   The absolute good being practically unattainable, at least as a social goal, due to the depth and diversity of human needs and aspirations, the limitations inherent in the world, and the consequent competition among men, our working objective must be the greatest *possible* good. And this, of course, will be nothing but the maximum possible satisfaction of men's goals, given men as they are and the world as we actually find it. Realizing that not every man will achieve what he wants, that a limited measure of happiness will necessarily be the lot of most, and that many needs are destined to pain and frustration, the practical objective of philosophy is to discover the general principles according to which as much as possible of men's passions and wants can find satisfaction and fulfillment, and at the least cost in terms of the denial or frustration of the rest.

Liberty   Whatever is necessary to the attainment of well-being or happiness is unqualifiedly good, not for its own sake, of course, but as a means. It would be absurd to say of some state, such as health, or the love and warmth of the family, or such other things as have been found to be the ingredients of happiness, that these are good, but that certain steps necessary to their attainment are without value.

In a general way we can say that the absence of obstacles or hindrances to the fulfillment of aim and desire is necessary to such fulfillment, this being, indeed, a tautology. The tautology yields, however, a straight-forward definition of *freedom* or *liberty* and has therefore a considerable significance, since political philosophy could hardly take more than infant steps without this idea.

Total and partial freedom   A man is *totally* free with respect to a course of action, provided there is no obstacle or hindrance whatever to his pursuing that course of action at will. If he can pursue it, but only in the face of obstacles or hindrances, then he is still free with respect to it, but not totally so; his freedom to do it is restricted, but not abolished. It is in this sense, for example, that in some societies men are free to become wealthy. The obstacles to their wealth are in some cases not insuperable, and yet they cannot become wealthy at will. And so it is with most aims; they are, at least sometimes, attainable, but seldom effortlessly.

Absolute freedom   A man is absolutely free, or his liberty is unqualified, if he is totally free with respect to any course of action whatsoever; or in other words, in case there is no hindrance whatever to his doing anything he pleases. Of course such freedom as that is rarely possessed by mortal men, and in fact never is; for in the case of that rare individual who might succeed in demolishing every conventional obstacle, there are still limita-tions imposed by nature herself. His mortality alone ensures this.

In the light of these definitions it is clear that a man might be free with respect to some actions and quite unfree with respect to others—something that is perfectly well known anyway. Thus, a man might be totally free to say some things, but not others; or free to write, but not to speak; or free to marry one woman, but not two; or free to walk, but not fly, and so on. No man on earth has ever been totally free with respect to everything, or in other words, absolutely free; but on the other hand, probably none has ever been in total bondage either, or in other words, such that there was not one single thing he was not totally prevented from doing. This is, indeed, the lot of all of us, that there is a realm of actions which nothing at all hinders or prevents us from doing, another which we are hindered but not totally prevented from doing, and a third which we are absolutely prevented from doing at all. *All* human freedom, accord-ingly, is the freedom of some kind of jail, be it a large one or a small one. The *degree* of a man's freedom is simply the scope of the first of these realms in relation to the second and third.

The obstacles to liberty   Freedom, I have said, is an unqualified good, being necessary for the attainment of any good whatever—unless, to be sure, one wants to take his chances, sitting by and doing nothing, and hoping that some of the world's blessings will be showered upon him.

Nothing can be good if it is unattainable, and the freedom to seek the fulfillment of need is nothing but the attainability of such satisfaction, or in other words, the lack of hindrance and obstacle to the pursuit of happiness.

There are two general kinds of such obstacles, one of which ha; only metaphysical or theological significance, and the other of which is central to political philosophy. The first can be called natural, and the other man-made or conventional. By a *natural* obstacle is meant any fact, other than some man-made one, that prevents or hinders a man from doing what he might otherwise want to do. Thus there is a natural obstacle to a man flying like a bird—he lacks wings. Similarly, a man born without hands is prevented from becoming a pianist, and men are prevented from bearing children, as women are prevented from siring them—not because such things are forbidden but because of obstacles of a natural kind.

Conventional obstacles, on the other hand, are man-made prohibitions and hindrances, i.e., rules of various kinds. Thus, while there are usually no natural obstacles, there are usually the most dreadfully effective conventional obstacles to a man's assaulting or killing his neighbor, stealing, simultaneously cohabiting with two or more spouses, discharging shotguns in crowded theaters, and so on. There is, in short, a conventional obstacle to whatever is effectively *prohibited by rule*. The connection between such prohibition and the freedom and goodness of which I have spoken is of course quite obvious.

Natural obstacles to freedom are clearly of no concern to social philosophy, though they might interest theology. There is no place a man can carry his complaint concerning those limitations that are imposed upon him, or his world, by nature—except, perhaps, to his creator. It is, for example, an obvious evil that a man cannot live free from sickness and pain, that he cannot perhaps live much longer than he does, or even forever—but such frustrations as these are not laid upon him by his fellows, but only by God. And since God's ways are unlikely to be altered by our philosophy, such natural obstacles need not concern us at all.

It is quite otherwise with conventional obstacles, for these are the very creation of men. What men have made, they can and sometimes should destroy. Since, moreover, every conventional obstacle diminishes an unqualified good—human freedom or the natural sovereignty every man has with respect to himself—and is therefore inherently evil, the question arises whether *every* such obstacle, or every conventional law or rule, should not be abolished. If not, then there is clearly needed some *justification* for the toleration of such evils; and such justification can only be the avoidance of even greater evils, in case any justification exists at all. Law, and particularly criminal law, is not in itself something good. On the contrary, it is an evil, since its immediate effect is to diminish the freedom that nature has given to everyone. The burden is therefore upon those who would have such law to show that the consequences of disposing of it would be worse than the inherent evil of conventional restraint. This is without doubt the first task of any political philosophy, for unless it can be done, the national course would appear to be the demolishment of law for the unfettered enjoyment of anarchy.

The Theory of Anarchy   VII

With the exception of those few creatures that have been domesticated and otherwise subjugated and caged by men (and whose natures have thereby been emasculated), human beings are the only creatures on earth that live under the galling constraint of government and the coercion of rules. All others enjoy unfettered freedom, not being constrained by rules and conventions but only by the obstacles that nature has placed in their paths. Government is a purely human fabrication and is intrinsically coercive and hence antithetical to freedom. To speak of free men living under the constraint of criminal law would seem to be a contradiction in terms, for such laws are prohibitions and are accordingly conventional obstacles to free action. A man who desires to do something—anything—but is prevented by a conventional or man-made rule from doing it, is to that extent unfree. It may be that there are good reasons why he should be thus constrained, even overwhelming reasons, but the presence of such reasons does not convert a constraint into its opposite. It is still a constraint, though perhaps a justified one. Absolute social freedom is the absence of any such hindrance that is purely conventional, such as law or custom. Clearly, then, only a lover of darkness and confusion can speak blithely of freedom under law or of free men in a governed society. It may be that governments and laws, and all the oppressive apparatus associated with these, are for some reason or other necessary. It may even be that governed men are relatively less unfree than they would be under certain appalling conditions of lawlessness and savagery that we can easily imagine, wherein obstacles more constraining than laws would be thrown in their paths. But let no one say without proof that law and government, as such, enhance human freedom when it seems to be their very nature to restrict it.

If freedom is an unqualified good, then the ideal societal state can be nothing but an anarchical one—a state of men living together without any conventional coercions whatever. Such an ideal societal state would be quite literally one of lawlessness, and the ideality of it is, of course, that only in such a state can men enjoy the unqualified goodness of freedom. The introduction of a single rule or law into such a state is the beginning of its corruption, for such a law can only serve to restrain someone from doing what he might otherwise want to do and can therefore only serve to divest him of an unqualified good, that is, of his freedom. It is worth noting, incidentally, that while Plato regarded the anarchical state as the penultimate stage of the corruption of the ideal state, the very opposite is suggested here. Anarchy is, at least abstractly, the ideal, and any departure from anarchy, by the introduction of coercive law, the corruption of that idea.

Given men as they are, then—that is, given that men are striving, appetitive, goal-seeking beings, and that in fact their needs and wants are vast beyond enumeration and intense beyond measure—we can ask: Under what conditions is anarchy a possible societal state?

The conditions of anarchy   There are two such conditions, both already alluded to, and either of which would be sufficient for anarchical social life.

The first would be an environment that contains such a plenitude of satisfactions, an environment so bountiful and benign, that no man would ever need to fear the slightest frustration of any aim he might have, great or small. If our world were like this no restraint would ever need to be placed on any man, for the satisfaction of his needs and desires would never involve the frustration of another man's; there would always be plenty of everything for both. Men would have no inclination to compete or struggle against each other, for the objectives of such competition or struggle would be effortlessly attainable without competition. If our world were like a vast and bountiful berry patch containing, say, only two berry pickers, there would be no need of rules to determine which berries should belong to whom and under what conditions, nor would there be any need of a supervisor to ensure a fair distribution of the berries in accordance with such rules. In such a world, anarchy could prevail without threat or danger, for without any need of rules, none would arise.

Of course our world is not like this and never will be. Our world is such that a man pursuing his goals is very likely to encounter others pursuing the same goals, or goals incompatible with his, and to perceive that their satisfactions can be attained only at the expense of his own. Men's paths do cross, and they discover themselves competing. In this real world the mere existence of a society—that is, of a multiplicity of men living in proximity to each other—provides a setting for conflict simply because the world is as it is, namely, limited. This condition of an anarchical society does not, therefore, offer much hope of fulfillment.

The second condition would be a human nature that is totally benevolent or loving. That is to say, there would be no need of any restraints upon any man if the solicitude of every man for his fellows matched his concern for himself. Why would there be any need for laws against theft if no man, however deprived, had ever the slightest inclination to steal? Why would there be any need for coercive law restraining men from assault if every man felt entirely secure with every other, even though that other were a total stranger? If, in short, human nature were such that every man could be entirely depended upon to do for everyone else whatever he would do for himself, and to refrain from doing to anyone what he would not do to himself, then there would be no need whatever of laws to coerce men in the direction of such behavior. Without the need of such laws, there would be no such laws, and the society of men would be one of lawlessness, or anarchy.

The lawlessness of minute bodies politic   Is such anarchy possible? On first consideration it seems not, but that is only because we think of society in a stereotyped way, as nothing less than a vast political state. But if we think of a society or body politic as any multiplicity of persons living together and sharing some sort of common life, then we do actually find anarchical societies in considerable number. A *family*, for example, is on this definition a body politic, though of course a minute one. It has an identifiable domain, the type of bond between its members that normally (though to a lesser degree) welds nations together, and ways of settling disputes which, ideally, involve no coercion. Moreover, a harmonious family is usually a society wherein total anarchy prevails precisely because the members of this society possess the requisite quality of lovingness. Thus the members of a family need not fear thefts from each other, for their mutual trust has been amply justified. They need not fear assault or fraud simply because one does not normally feel inclined to assault or defraud another whom he deeply loves. Police officers armed with rules and coercive power are not needed around the household to spy, ferret out, and punish attempts by some members to injure and take advantage of the others, for these members can effectively rely upon each other for the avoidance of such injury. The deep love that people have for each other, when they do have such love, prevents mutual injury far more effectively than coercive law, by overcoming the very inclination toward it.

It is worth noting that we have lately witnessed the rebirth of another type of anarchical society, though one which is, like the human family, a minute one. We refer here to the commune, consisting of a multiplicity of people living together without coercive laws and sometimes styling itself a "family," though blood relationships may be entirely absent. Here, too, there is an identifiable domain and certain bonds that unite the members into a genuine society, rather than a mere plurality of persons who share the same roof. In these cases such bonds are usually shared aspirations or common philosophical or religious convictions. Here again, then, it is entirely possible for a number of persons otherwise unrelated to join together in a society that is united, not by coercive law, but by love. The members of such a society may, though they need not, own things in common, more or less in the manner of a natural family; but what is distinctive about it is that their relationships to each other are governed only by a few rules that are commonly agreed to, and the adherence to those rules is ensured, not by threat, but by love. Rules, in such a society, have more the form of custom than law and resemble gentle manners and the practices men adopt for agreeable social intercourse, rather than constraints. In such a society the very maximum of freedom obtains, but without undermining the security of each member from injury from his fellows.

A state of anarchy or absolute liberty is therefore possible, given the world and men precisely as they are, but only on a minute scale. Within a family one may leave his belongings lying about without fear of theft and turn his back to the others without the remotest fear of assault, but it is far otherwise when he ventures forth into those larger bodies politic which we call the city, the province, the state. Here one can by no means be sure that the man behind his back intends him no harm, that his goods will not be coveted and, at the first opportunity, seized, for the love that bathes the home life cannot be assumed to exist outside in any sufficient force to abolish all concern a man may have for his safety. In the larger society, in which the love of man is weaker, something else is needed in its stead, and this something else can of course be nothing but laws of restraint. There is needed, in short, the coercive force of government. Where love is wanting, freedom must be compromised in the sheer interest of safety. Abstractly considered, it is possible that the day might come when the utopia that actually exists in the ideal and sometimes real family circle will become sufficiently comprehensive to include much larger societies; but there is not the slightest sign that such a day is near, and there are perpetual reminders that the greed, vice, and callousness of our race are as durable as the race itself. This is enough to ensure that the age of anarchy, if it is to be anything better than pure savagery, will never come. The deprivation of freedom, the corruption of the anarchical state, is of course a great evil, being the deprivation of an unqualified good; but it is a necessary one, for the threat to body, life, and property that otherwise flourishes in every quarter is a greater evil still, being the threat of frustration of *every* aim and purpose.

The Defense of Anarchy VIII

There has recently appeared a defense of political anarchy on grounds totally different from any alluded to here, in Robert Wolff's brilliant essay, *In Defense of Anarchism.* * One finds in it nothing at all concerning human needs and the means to their satisfaction, nothing concerning the considerations of security, the mutual threat that men living in proximity to each other present, nothing, even, concerning the common good or the pursuit of happiness, or any considerations whether the criminal law is necessary to the attainment of it. The defense of the doctrine of anarchy rests, instead, on an abstract principle of metaphysical ethics, referred to by its author (borrowing from Kant) as "autonomy." It is to his autonomy, we are told, that every man owes his dignity, his moral worth as a man, and his responsibility as a moral agent, at least in the sense that if he is divested of it by any ruler, or even voluntarily surrenders it, or loses it otherwise, then he is thereby also deprived of his moral responsibility, his dignity, and those other qualities dear to clergymen and moralists of an earlier age.

Autonomy and command It is a purely abstract argument and it is totally conclusive. Autonomy is defined in such a way that *all* government, the best as well as the worst, and regardless of whether it is voluntarily embraced or thrust upon one, is automatically rendered incompatible with it. Autonomy is, briefly, that state of being the sole author of one's actions

* New York: Harper & Row, Publishers, 1970.

46

and thus subject to no command, and government is described as the power to command. Obviously it is not going to be hard to show that autonomy and government, thus conceived, are incompatible. And since such autonomy is declared to be essential to a man's dignity, worth, and moral responsibility, it logically follows that no form of government is compatible with these. Therefore no government, which this author equates with a state, can have any moral justification. One might of course offer the alternative thesis, familiar from some of the classical philosophers, that some sacrifice of one's autonomy is justified in order to obtain the security and perhaps other blessings that good government sometimes makes possible, but this author blocks that line of thought at the very outset. No one, he says, *can* voluntarily give up his autonomy, for this would be to yield to another one's responsibility for his own actions, which is impossible. He, and he alone, possesses this or can possess it. If on the other hand one does not thus voluntarily submit to another but is subjugated to him by superior power, then he does not thereby surrender his autonomy but has it wrested from him. The emergence of government by this means is of course a familiar and baneful story, but it hardly constitutes a justification of such rule. It suggests, in fact, the exact opposite.

In outline, then, the position is this: No man can surrender his autonomy; every form of government is incompatible with the autonomy of those governed; therefore, no form of government is justified or legitimate. The conclusion can be otherwise expressed this way: Every state that exists is the *de facto* but wrongful exercise of power. The state that exists by right is impossible.

The essay does not at all concern itself with this inference, nor does it try to justify its presupposition, which is simply proclaimed and iterated. Instead, its author examines in turn various governmental forms, all variants upon the formula of democratic government, and shows (very easily, since it is a logical consequence) that each and every one of them involves the compromise of a man's autonomy and is therefore, he concludes, to be rejected.

Clearly, we must look much more closely at the instrument by which this result is obtained, at that great lever with which all government is so effortlessly overturned. Is it as large as it is claimed to be? To find out, we must do what the author himself does not do; we must examine the presupposition of the whole system, abstractly referred to as "autonomy." It is not enough simply to proclaim this, within the framework of large and comfortable notions of morality for which men have a customary reverence, and then expect the world to bow to it. We have to ask, *Is* there such a thing? Or is it nothing but the creation and plaything of abstract metaphysical ethics?

The concept of autonomy   To describe a man as "autonomous" is to say that he is *rational* and *free* with respect to his own conduct. His *rationality*, in this context, consists of his deliberative capacity, his ability to consider reasons for his actions, to weigh the pros and cons of his choices before he makes them. And his *freedom* consists of his ability to act in the light of those reasons. The two together—that is, rationality and freedom—confer upon him his *moral responsibility* for his behavior. The concepts of moral responsibility and autonomy are thus coextensive, each being necessary and sufficient for the other. Autonomous men, then, are morally responsible men. They can also be described, in the manner of Kant, as self-legislating —as beings who act freely in accordance with "laws" that are derived from their own reason.

Who, then, is not autonomous? Most manifestly, children and madmen, either because they lack the rationality requisite for evaluating the considerations in the light of which they are to act, or because they lack the freedom to act from such considerations, being governed instead by impulses or other irrational forces. Or of course they may lack both.

Excepting, then, children and madmen, are all other men autonomous? Clearly not. The slave, for example, lacks the requisite freedom. Though he may by his reason see his duty, he may be prevented from doing it by whoever determines his actions. He is the clearest example of one who is not self-legislating.

Who else? Well, having got to this point, we now see that *no* one is autonomous who is subject to the command of another. For to the extent that my actions are in response to another's commands, then to that extent they are not my actions, or at least, not actions that are rational and free. They are accordingly not actions for which I am responsible, and I am not autonomous. An autonomous man can, to be sure, heed another's command—the command of any legislator, for example—and he may then be led to do as commanded, but not simply *because* it is commanded. Rather, because he himself sees the reason for acting that way and freely does so. In this case what is presented as a command is in fact not a command at all to the person to whom it is directed, but is instead a persuasion to which he freely assents without sacrifice of his autonomy. Strictly speaking, there can *be* no such thing as a command in the eyes of an autonomous person; for to the extent that one acts because commanded to, to that extent he does not act autonomously—that is, rationally and freely.

The problem of political philosophy, therefore, as this author sees it, is that of discovering some form of government wherein those governed can (1) be subject to its authority (to its commands as expressed in law), and yet (2) be autonomous. It is fairly easy to see that there can be no such governmental form. Even a representative democracy, for example, involves the enforced obedience of citizens to commands that they did not enunciate, these being instead the creation of their "representatives." Nor does rule by the majority work, for all those in the minority are by that system deprived of their autonomy. Such a citizen, having considered reasons, deliberated, and then chosen his course of action, may find himself compelled by the superior force of the majority to do otherwise, perhaps to do the exact opposite of what he had decided upon. Nor can we even find hope in a system of unanimous direct democracy wherein every law would require, for its validity as law, the consent of everyone to whom it applies. Under such a system every citizen would be his own lawgiver as his autonomy requires, since he would be bound by no law or command to which he did not assent. Such a "state" or government would be indistinguishable, however, from the absence of any government at all, or in other words, indistinguishable from anarchy; for a law that is rendered null and void by the mere noncompliance of a single person is no law, and a government resting upon such a foundation would not be a government that could survive to the end of the day it was established.

Government, then, whatever may be its form, whether it be a liberal and popular democracy or the most arbitrary despotism, whether or not it enjoys the allegiance of those governed, whether it is benevolent or exploitive, whether it reduces its citizens to poverty and wretchedness or, on the contrary, brings within their reach all the blessings of culture and civilized life, is in any case, and notwithstanding whatever may be truly said in praise of it, *illegitimate*. There can only be *de facto* states that exercise supreme power over those governed. There can be no *de jure* state that exercises such power by right. The obstacle to such a state is simple and clear: it is incompatible with someone's autonomy.

Three basic questions We need now to answer three questions, never raised in this strange book, but simply taken for granted. The first is whether moral responsibility does require this unqualified autonomy. The second is whether autonomy, thus conceived, is a desirable thing to possess. And the third is whether there is such a thing as autonomy in the first place, or in other words, whether men by nature are, in the senses required, rational and free.

The answer to the first question is doubtless affirmative; in traditional philosophy there is a notion of moral responsibility, equivalent to moral praiseworthiness and blameworthiness, which does presuppose both the rationality and freedom of anyone to whom it is thought to apply. It is a concept that came into philosophy by way of Christian theology. It is foreign to the moral philosophies of ancient Greece, though with a few shifts of emphasis it can be read into Socratic thought. At the hands of Kant and other rationalist thinkers it came to be separated from the presuppositions of religion and incorporated in abstract or metaphysical ethics as something allegedly discoverable by reason. Blame, in this uniquely moral sense, is always cancelled by the claim that the agent could not help doing what he did, and equally by the claim that he did not know any better or did not understand why he should not. This is simply abstract ethics that involves the relationships of certain concepts to each other. There is nothing in such a system to show that anyone ever has been morally responsible in that sense, for the conceptual relations would be unaltered by any proof that, for example, no really free action has ever been performed in the history of mankind.

It is clear, however, that this observation proves nothing whatever about the propriety or desirability of anarchy. The most it shows is that there may be, or indeed doubtless is, an incompatibility between certain familiar and traditional philosophical notions—moral responsibility and enforced command, in the present case. From this it cannot be concluded, without raising the remaining two questions, that there can be no authority for any state to govern, for we have no reason to assert that men are responsible in the special sense required, aside from the fact that this opinion has been widely held by Christian theologians and by Kant. Nor have we as yet any reason to suppose it would be desirable that men should be responsbile, in this philosophical sense.

Are men, then, free and rational, in the senses required for autonomy? Or perhaps in fairness the question should be phrased: Were it not for the corruption introduced by political life, would men by nature possess such freedom and rationality?

This is, at least, enormously doubtful. There is no way of proving that men have "free will" or that their behavior is even normally governed by a consideration of reason, and there are certainly very many strong reasons for doubting both, particularly the first. No philosopher has ever shown that men are free in this metaphysical sense; indeed, about the only argument one ever finds for this in philosophy is that if they were not, then they would not be morally responsible for their actions! Such a reflection is of no use in this context.

What we actually find in the world is that men act, generally, from certain inclinations, desires, and sometimes, strong passions. It is extraordinarily rare for anyone to pretend that these were rationally chosen, particularly in the cases of persons other than themselves. Men are basically what the world has made them, and particularly those of their fellow men who have had an overwhelming influence upon them, such as their parents. It is all these forces, beginning in infancy, that seem to determine totally what a given man will prize, what he will deem worth striving for, what he will dread, and above all, what he will feel shame and guilt about—in short, what will incline him to feel, think, and act as he does. To imagine that one can preserve or even acquire an "autonomy" in the face of what is thus generally known of the manner in which each of us comes to be what he is is hardly short of heroic. It is to substitute, in the place of the human beings we live with and deal with and try more or less to get on with as best we can, a bloodless, odorless, and brainless abstraction, loftily assaying reasons, deliberating, making moral choices, hearkening to duty as conveyed by his practical reason, thereby preserving his "dignity" and his autonomy, and through all, having less resemblance to anything that was ever called a human being than to some metaphysical fiction.

Some illustrations   To bring this whole matter quite clearly into the realm of fact, into the world that we suppose ourselves to be talking about, let us imagine ourselves for a moment surveying some vast prison population, of the sort that can usually be found not far from where one happens to be sitting at any time of his life. What shall we say of these? That they are free and rational agents who were accustomed to deliberating prior to choice, weighing the pros and cons of various alternatives under consideration, and then finally choosing freely whatever courses of action they undertook, including those that led them to their present deplorable condition? Are they autonomous beings who obey laws of their own creation and thus preserve both their moral responsibility and their dignity? Such a way of viewing the matter is *possible,* though difficult even for the moral philosopher if actually confronted with such a situation.

Or should we then perhaps say that these living, feeling, striving men before us are rather like ourselves, the products of the influences to which they have been subjected from birth, differing from us not so much in the wickedness of their rational choices and the perversity of their wills, as in the baneful influences which it was their lot to be cast under? Certainly everything we *know* of human nature suggests that something like this is the true general picture. In order to fill in the details of how any man comes to be what he is, it is very doubtful whether anyone, whether he be a psychologist, criminologist, or philosopher, would ever require such notions as the autonomy or freedom of the will, deliberate or rational choice, moral responsibility, or any of the similar notions that fill moralists, together with clergymen of an earlier generation, with such comfort.

Should it be said, then, that a prison yard was a poor place to look for autonomous men? Children and madmen had already been excluded from this community; perhaps felons should have been excluded too.

We next station ourselves, then, where we can watch the progress of a civil riot, with a full view of the looting, arson, general destruction, and mayhem. We suppose that there are in this picture neither children, madmen, nor criminals. Which description shall we now apply? The one drawn from a theory of metaphysical morals, beginning with the notions of the free will, rational choice, autonomy, and so on? Or should we refer instead to drives, fears, resentments, anxieties, and so on?

But perhaps a riot is likewise not the most promising place to search for specimens of autonomous men, crowned with that dignity that can be bestowed only by the capacity for rational deliberation and a free will. Let us then station ourselves above the street of any city at midday, or at any great crossroad, and observe the coming and going of masses of human beings, each on some mission or other, each driven by some impulse— in some cases greed, in others love, in others anxiety, in still others hope, and so on through the inventory of the passions. And now again we ask, not with reference to some preconceived rational man whose image exists in the thought of the philosophical moralist, but with reference to the very throng that is before us, whether their behavior would be best understood in such terms as rational, free, and deliberate choice, or in terms more familiar to an elementary psychology. Why, for example, do they rush in such numbers into this store and that? Why, when it begins to rain, do a hundred umbrellas go up, as if in response to some unheard command? Why, when there is pushing and shoving, is it met with abusive language? When the hand of a policeman goes up, why do twenty cars stop? And why, when a blind man appears with his tapping cane, does every car stop, as if at a signal?

Describe what is seen in as much detail as you please, and then ask this: Why do actual men behave in these ways? Are these the courses of action decided upon by rational deliberation and the exercise of a free will? Or are they rather the responses of men conditioned to a civilized life?

Perhaps there is no way of proving that the concepts of rationality, free will, responsibility, and autonomy are of little use in the understanding of human conduct, but it can hardly be said that they have shed much light on these matters to date other than to supply the conceptual context needed by religion and rationalistic ethics for the ascription of moral praise and blame. But if that is not one's purpose, and if, for example, one is instead inquiring concerning some sort of justification for a social and political life and seeking useful criteria for the evaluation of alternative political institutions, it is difficult to see how such notions drawn from abstract ethics even enter the picture.

That there is or ever has been such a thing as an "autonomous" man is at least doubtful, and the author of the essay under consideration nowhere attempts the slightest proof of it. That we have any such autonomy *by nature* is extremely doubtful. Such a thesis would surely belong only to

a kind of fabulous anthropology. It is a thing adored by academic philosophers who share with Hume the wonderful capacity to thread their way
through abstractions of their own creation in their studies, but leave them
all behind the moment they step past their doors and into the world. Such
rationality as we possess, together with the capacity to think and to deliberate, to choose and to act as free men, seems to be the *product* of civilized
life, which is to say, of a politically governed life that has had a very considerable historical development, and there is no reason whatever to think
that such qualities emerge only within democratic .institutions. Far, then,
from being incompatible with government, even with despotic government, rationality appears, historically, to be itself its product.

It is then fair to say, I believe, that the autonomous man displayed
in the essay before us is hardly more than the fabrication of abstract
philosophy, and the kind of manikin upon whom the rationalistic moralist
tries various concepts—in the present case, the concept of government—to
see how they fit. In this case the fit is found to be very bad, altogether too
tight, and no matter how the garment is cut and enlarged and altered in
numberless ways, it is just never going to fit, as was made perfectly clear
at the outset. And so, wonderously, it is decided to preserve the manikin
and cast out government, the very best as well as the very worst, as un-
worthy of any allegiance.

The uselessness of this idea   There still remains the question, however,
whether such autonomy, whether it exists or not, would be anything very
desirable, whether anyone would be much the worse off for being born
without it, for instance, and never acquiring it. And with respect to this
question it must be confessed that autonomy seems very much like the
human soul. Here is something every man is supposed to prize above
everything else, because it gives him his worth and dignity and thus ele-
vates him above the rest of creation (though perhaps not above madmen
and children), something whose loss would be an incalculable evil—and
yet something about which hardly anyone seems able to form any clear
notion at all. As autonomy appears to supply the medium for the ascription of moral praise and blame, the soul seems to have no other function
than to serve as a peg on which to hang various theological teachings.
Both are declared precious beyond measure, the one by rationalist ethics,
the other by rationalist theology, and yet neither ever enters descriptively
into any of the sciences of human nature.

The autonomy of a man, as embodied in but a single person, is declared to have an uncompromisable worth sufficient for overturning every
government. Let us, then, test this alleged worth. To do so we can concoct
in our imaginations a person who is clearly devoid of such autonomy, who
is imaginatively created to be without it, but who nevertheless has certain

other qualities compatible with this deficiency, and we can then ask ourselves whether someone so conceived is not better than an animal, madman, or child.

We suppose, then, someone who is in a word born sweet—not sweet by choice, but by nature. This is the person with a warm and loving heart who gives help to anyone in pain and suffering whenever possible, wherever needed, not as the result of a free choice, but simply as the expression of a compassionate nature. This compassionate nature, we can plausibly suppose, was itself the result of a wise choice of parents; that is, he was born into a warm and loving family who lavished love upon him and thereby made him to become what he is. One cannot be in his presence for long without sensing his warmth, for his smiles are effortless and sincere, unplanned, unchosen, virtual reflexes, and he seems accompanied almost by the light of heaven. Whatever he does stirs approbation in those who see it, not because it is heroic or done in response to any sense of duty or right, but simply because it has the mark of that love for the world by which this man's life is unreflectively guided.

But he lacks that gift of autonomy. His will is not free, but in virtual if not total bondage to his feelings and inclinations. He neither reasons nor deliberates, but simply responds, as though to an instinct, whenever the occasion for sweet compassion presents itself.

Shall we say he is without worth or dignity, no better than an animal, madman, or child? We can indeed say that he is without autonomy, and even that he is neither morally praiseworthy nor blameworthy because he is simply acting from his nature and not from rational choice. But no one who is not intoxicated with the roundhouse declarations of rationalist ethics could say that he is without worth; nor would anyone enunciate any absurdity if he were to declare such a man to be in fact the ideal of human nature, who rises as near as mortals can to the radiance of the angels. His lack of autonomy appears to detract not in the least from that judgment.

We can at least then say it is *doubtful* whether there is such a thing as human autonomy and *doubtful* whether it makes much difference to our worth as human beings. It therefore has not really been proved that there has never been and will never be any government that has a justification for its existence. Whatever may be the proper limit of governmental authority and the true principle of liberty, the former cannot be reduced to zero nor the latter expanded without limit. The problem of the degree to which citizens may legitimately be coerced by the state is perhaps the most important problem in political philosophy, but the answer to it cannot be that no such coercion whatever is permissible.

The Classical Defense of Liberty IX

The problem of liberty is first of all a problem concerning the creation of criminal law—the prohibitory part of the law that attaches penalties to certain behavior. Civil law is related to liberty in a quite different way, generally providing the means to the ends people seek, rather than restricting them through the definition of crimes.

Thus, legislation involves many things, some of overwhelming importance. It is through legislation that agents of government spread poisons over our land, killing insects and, of course, birds and fish; that they despoil our fields and forests to build big highways; they also build and equip universities, care for the poor, regulate industry, communications, and so on, endlessly. But legislation of this kind, important as it is, does not bear directly on the problem of liberty. We shall instead be concerned with legislation, the explicit (and not the incidental) object of which is to regulate conduct. This is law that defines felonies, misdemeanors and offenses.

Our first question, then, comes to this: To what extent is such legislation justified? Is it justified at all? Since all such law delimits the natural freedom of the individual, is any such law proper? If so, then by what principle, if any? Is there any conduct which may *not* properly be forbidden by law? If, for example, assault may properly be forbidden under threat by the state, may not also the wearing of strange dress, the desecration of symbols, the eating of shellfish or insects, and so on? At what line, if any, may we draw the reasonable limits of social freedom and those of criminal legislation?

It is widely thought that this question was answered once and for all by John Stuart Mill, and that all that is needed henceforth is an appreciation of his grand principle of liberty and an understanding of the invincible arguments by which he defended it. Even men of such sophisticated legal and philosophical thought as H. L. A. Hart suppose that Mill has defined the principle of liberty, and that his successors need only to expound and defend it.* Hardly any students pass through college without having read the famous essay *On Liberty*, and the prevailing view is that it leaves little more to be said.

This is not so. Mill's essay is a declamation and not a cogent philosophical treatise. As an ideological tract it is, perhaps, inspiring. Some can perhaps derive from it a certain attitude, a certain partisan feeling for freedom, an appreciation of philosophy in the service of a noble cause; but one does not in fact find there a coherent principle of liberty. Our first task will be to establish that point and then try to supply the answer for which Mill was groping.

The failure of Mill's principle   It will not be necessary to review the whole of Mill's *On Liberty* because the error in it is central and can be exhibited at once. Essentially it is this: That the principle of liberty, as Mill formulates it, can be used in support of *any* criminal legislation whatsoever. No law, however oppressive or frivolous, really violates it. And clearly, a "principle" of liberty that is not violated by *any* legislation or practice is not a principle at all. It is only a vague and meaningless exhortation.

Mill's formulation   Mill expressed his central thesis in these words:

> . . . *the sole end for which mankind are warranted, individually or collectively, in interfering with the liberty of action of any of their number, is self-protection* (p. 956).**

The principle is expressed by Mill in other ways, which he evidently took to be simply alternative ways of saying the same thing, but which in fact render the thing totally ambiguous. Thus, to the foregoing he immediately adds:

* See H. L. A. Hart, *Law, Liberty and Morality* (New York: Vintage Books, Random House & Alfred A. Knopf, Inc., 1963).
** All quotations are from *English Philosophers from Bacon to Mill*, ed. E. A. Burtt (New York: Random House, Inc., 1939).

THE CLASSICAL DEFENSE OF LIBERTY

> *. . . the only purpose for which power can be rightfully exercised over any member of a civilized community, against his will, is to prevent harm to others* (Ibid.).

and then further, that to justify applying compulsion to anyone

> *the conduct from which it is desired to deter him must be calculated to produce evil to someone else* (Ibid.).

And on the next page Mill expresses his principle one more way by saying

> *there is a sphere of action in which society, as distinguished from the individual, has, if any, only an indirect interest; comprehending all that portion of a person's life and conduct which affects only himself, or if it also affects others, only with their free, voluntary, and undeceived consent and participation* (p. 957).

Elsewhere in his essay Mill offers still other formulations of this basic idea, but none, I think, which removes the defect contained in these.

That defect is not the falsity of the principle as variously formulated. Certainly the upholder of freedom nods approval of the sentiment expressed in these declarations. The defect is rather that no coherent principle has been formulated. That is to say, if one is seeking a philosophical principle that defines the proper line of governmental and societal interference in the life of the individual, then he does not find it here, for no such line has been drawn at all. A government, however free or despotic, could draw that line in any manner it might choose, and then in complete consistency cite Mill's principle to justify the result.

The narrow interpretation of "harm"   To see this, consider the crucial expressions "self-protection," "harm to others," and "evil to someone else." What, for instance, does *harm to another* consist in? Shall we construe this narrowly, limiting it, say, to bodily injury? Of course not, for the principle would then not allow for protection from such things as theft and fraud. A man could walk off with all his neighbor's livestock and, if charged with overstepping the bounds of liberty, point out in complete truth that he had inflicted no bodily injury on anyone and had, therefore, on Mill's principle as thus construed, harmed no one. Construing the notion of *harm* in this narrow way has the immediate consequence of expanding individual liberty far beyond any reasonable limit and leaves us free to commit any offense to others that falls short of bodily injuring them. *Harming* and *injuring* must accordingly encompass much more than just *wounding*.

The wider interpretation of "harm"   If, to overcome the difficulty just cited, we construe the idea of harm more broadly, we find that the principle becomes so restrictive as to permit no real freedom whatever. If we say, for example, that *harming* a man consists not merely of injury to his body, but to any of his deepest interests, then of course we bring such things as theft and fraud within its meaning. Men do have a deep interest in the security of their property as well as of their persons. But unfortunately, men have *other* deep interests as well which no believer in freedom supposes for a minute should never be foiled.

Thus, there are men who have a deep interest in such things as religion, patriotism, public manners, the preservation of wildlife, and so on, without end. Now if we say that no one shall be permitted to do anything that would foil, frustrate, or damage any such interest held by anyone, this will be about equivalent to saying that no one may do anything at all. The whole of the criminal law would be summed up in saying that all actions are prohibited. And a principle having that consequence can hardly be called a principle of liberty.

An example   Consider a village whose life centers about the practice of religion. Such villages can still be found in the remoter reaches of Quebec. And now let us suppose that someone settles himself down in that village with the avowed and determined mission of doing all he can, through spoken and written persuasion, to unsettle the religion of these villagers, undermine their faith, and break the grip of the Church upon them. Concerning such a state of affairs we can certainly say, *first*, that if this village is in fact a free society, then this iconoclast can by no means be prevented from pursuing his destructive mission with all industry and vigor, assuming, of course, that his instruments are those of persuasion and not physical violence; and *second*, that such activity on his part nevertheless *hurts* the villagers, in the sense of "hurts" that is now before us. That is, it does most manifestly frustrate and damage a deep interest of its members, or is at least calculated to. Indeed, it is not hard to imagine that their resentment of such activity might be greater than if this outsider undertook to steal all their cattle.

Mill's principle, as thus literally interpreted, does not work, for if it is applied to such a society, with a broad interpretation placed upon the crucial concept of "hurting others," the immediate result is the destruction of the most elementary liberties anyone could claim, such as freedom in the expression of theological opinion. When we consider that there are narrow-minded people (and in fact whole societies of them) who have a deep interest in such things as uniformity of manners and dress, sabbatarian observances, respect for traditional cultural values, and so on, and feel deeply injured by deviations from these, we see how little protection of individual liberty is provided by Mill's principle.

Alternative formulations of the principle   In none of his formulations does Mill ever appear to overcome this difficulty. It seems inherent in the principle itself. Thus, when he insists that the liberty of the individual encompasses "all that portion of a person's life and conduct which affects only himself" (p. 957), and that within that realm an individual should be left alone, the obvious response is that no such portion of one's life and conduct exists. *Everything* one does, though it may be no more than the expression of an opinion sincerely held or the display of eccentric manners or dress, affects others. Nor does it do any good to add, as Mill does, that in case one's conduct affects others, this must be "only with their free, voluntary, and undeceived consent and participation." Reverting to our example of the pious village, it is no principle of liberty that the villagers must freely and voluntarily *consent* to the expression of offensive opinions as a condition of their being enunciated. This is exactly equivalent to saying that every opinion to which anyone objects may be legitimately silenced, without in any way infringing the freedom of the speaker. And this is absurd.

The difficulty is clearly insuperable. Either such expressions as "hurting others," "protection," "affecting others," or "evil to others" are given a narrow interpretation, or they are not. If interpreted narrowly, then men must, in the name of freedom, be permitted to do whatever they please, short of physically assaulting their fellows. But if not interpreted narrowly, then men may, in accordance with Mill's principle, be restrained in the most elementary expressions of freedom such as the expression of opinion or even the display of manners or the pursuit of life styles offensive to others. So however the principle is understood, the result is absurd.

Effects of Mill's formulation upon his own philosophy   This difficulty sometimes infects Mill's development of his own ideas, occasionally with serious result. For example, he decides, in the light of his principle, that a man who chooses a life of idleness may be judicially punished in case his idleness affects others adversely—his family, for example. Should we not observe that there are very few men whose idleness, were they to choose it, would not adversely affect someone, perhaps seriously? Mill draws the same conclusion with respect to such things as drunkenness and extravagance. One is free to be a drunk provided this does not adversely affect others. What others? And how adversely? Mill specifically mentions one's children and one's creditors—but having mentioned these, at what point shall we stop? Shall we include representatives of the Christian Temperance League? If not, why not? Indeed, the whole principle virtually explodes in its author's face when he finds that it permits the judicial restraint of those whose styles of conduct are "offenses against decency" and "violations of good manners," and draws the appropriate inference (p. 1027) that such behavior should indeed be suppressed! Clearly, this is no principle of liberty at all, but an instrument for grinding men down to conform to someone's conception of "decency" and "good manners."

At one point Mill declares that every man should observe a certain line of conduct toward others, such conduct consisting, he says, of "not injuring the interests of one another" (p. 1008). What interests? The interests these others may have in such things as decency and good manners? As if detecting the difficulty here, Mill adds the qualification, "or rather, certain interests, which, either by express legal provision or by tacit understanding, ought to be considered as rights." At the beginning of his essay, however, Mill had forsworn any appeal to the idea of an abstract right (p. 957). But quite apart from this, the qualification hardly helps, for "express legal provision" can be made for the prohibition of any practice whatever, and "tacit understanding" can similarly extend to anything—to bad manners, for example. Nor is the difficulty overcome by Mill's appeal, elsewhere (p. 1023), to the opinion of society concerning what it considers requisite for its protection. Uniformity of theological opinion, for example, as well as obeisance to the flag and other trappings of the state, have been and in fact still are thought by some societies to be requisite for their protection. Again we have, then, no principle of liberty here at all, but a slogan that can be put to any use one wishes, either for the expansion or the abolishment of individual freedom.

The need for a clear principle   Still, the problem Mill dealt with—which is nothing less than the age-old problem of liberty—is one of overwhelming importance. What Mill tried and failed to do is still desperately in need of being done. We do need a philosophical principle of liberty, one that is coherent and meaningful and, above all, one that does not merely presuppose the very distinctions it is intended to make. It is no principle of liberty, for example, to say that every man should have the right to do what he wishes, provided he does not infringe on the rights of others— for that only defines the idea of an individual right by presupposing it and leaves us with absolutely nothing. What is needed is a statement of what men's rights ought to be in a free society, and such a statement is not going to tell us much if it assumes the concept of a right, undefined and unexplained.

The True Principle of Liberty

X

If, as we have suggested, anarchy is the ideal societal state, but one that is impossible except on a relatively minute scale and under special circumstances of the kind considered earlier, it follows that the corruption of this ideal must be minimal if the maximum goodness possible is to be obtained. Or in other words, since the restriction of any man's freedom by coercive law is an unqualified evil, then no man's freedom should be restricted more than is necessary for the avoidance of even greater evil. On what principle, then, is it permissible to thus restrict human freedom—that is, to generate coercive criminal laws?

There can, properly, be only one such principle, the very one formulated by Mill—namely, the prevention of injury. The almost universal practice of mingling other principles with this one—such as that of fostering what is right or moral and suppressing what is wicked or immoral, or even that of promoting what is good, and generally acknowledged to be good, for everyone—is utterly improper and hateful to anyone who has a sense of the precious nature of freedom.

But of course what is needed at this point is a more precise account of *injury* than Mill ever undertook, for as we have seen, *any* act that anyone has ever had the slightest inclination to legislate against can be represented as injurious in some sense to someone.

The precise nature of injury There appear to be only three ways in which men can properly be said to injure each other, and these are: (1)

assault, (2) theft, and (3) fraud. Actions of these kinds can be called, borrowing from the terminology of law, *mala in se,* or actions that are bad in themselves. This is not, of course, the meaning the expression has in law, but it is useful in suggesting that nothing that is not an assault, theft, or fraud can be bad by its very nature. The expression thus helps to focus our attention upon real evils, and not things that are evil only because conventionally declared to be so. No man, for example, needs to be taught that an assault upon himself is something bad, nor does anyone suppose that the evil of such an action is a mere consequence of some edict, declaration, or law. It is bad in itself, and the same is true of theft and fraud.

All three terms should be construed fairly broadly, but not so broadly as to include everything that anyone happens to dislike. Thus a violent blow to a man is, of course, an assault—but so is deliberately driving him mad by forcing him to swallow a dangerous drug or something of that sort. Similarly, depriving a man of his property by spreading lies about him can be thought of as a species of theft, being essentially no different from physical divestment or seizure of his goods. Or again, seduction by means of false promises appears to be a form of fraud, though it might not ordinarily be so described. Among the things that are *not* to be counted as injuries are mere offenses to taste or sensibility. The use of unconventional and even offensive language, for example, is not by itself an assault, theft, or fraud, nor are eccentric styles of dress and grooming, however much some of these may be detested. Injury must mean something fairly definite and cannot be expanded to include everything under the sun that this or that man may wish to abolish. Otherwise there will really be no principle of legislation at all, other than that of prohibiting what someone happens not to like, which is really the abandonment of principle altogether.

It is not enough, as we have seen, to say with Mill that men may properly be restrained from acting in ways likely to injure others, unless one then spells out what is to be regarded as *injury.* If we limit the notion to personal injury, then we find that a free society must tolerate theft under Mill's principle, so that a man could walk off with his neighbor's cattle and burn all his buildings and still escape any charge of having injured him. If, on the other hand, we expand the notion of injury to include theft, should we not expand it still further to include eccentricity of life-style, the use of offensive language, disrespect for cherished symbols, irreligion, and so on, ad infinitum? Surely there are people who would, for example, be more injured by having their theological beliefs shattered by arguments than by having their very buildings shattered by bombs; and the very sight and sound of unconventional dress and language has more than once moved men to fierce retaliation and bloodshed, which indicates in the clearest way possible the existence of felt injury. How, then, can we declare some such injuries to be innocent actions and properly protected by law, in the name of liberty, and others not? Having decided that no man is entitled to assault, steal, or defraud, why shall we not then add: Nor to offend, distress, and upset?

Natural and conventional injury The answer to this serious problem lies, it is suggested, in a distinction between what may be called *natural* as opposed to *conventional* injury. The basic distinction between nature (*physis*) and convention (*nomos*) was drawn by the Greeks at about the time of Socrates, but the notion of injury has probably never been thus divided. It is a readily understood distinction, enormously useful to philosophy and jurisprudence, and it appears to be just the one that is needed here.

A *natural* injury is anything that evokes more or less deep resentment on the part of him who is injured, by virtue of his very nature as a man. A *conventional* injury, on the other hand, is what one resents, not just by virtue of his humanity but because of what he has learned, or how he has been conditioned by his culture. Ordinarily, those actions that are resented by rather few, and disregarded or even positively welcomed by others, are merely conventional injuries, whereas actions that are everywhere resented, at least by most men, are likely to be natural injuries.

The eating of pork, for example, or the disregard of certain sabbatarian observances, or the desecration of religious or patriotic symbols such as rosary beads, flags, and the like, are clearly conventional injuries. That there are men who deeply resent such acts, men who are, in fact, very clearly injured by them, shows only that these acts are injurious. It does not show that they are more than conventionally such. There are doubtless men who would, for instance, more deeply resent seeing their flag spat upon than being spat upon themselves, and who would even risk their safety to prevent it. But such an injury, however deep, is still no more than conventional. The same may of course be said of all injuries arising from eccentric life-styles, uncommon and thus "offensive" language, unorthodox habits of diet, dress, and so on.

On the other hand, injuries resulting from blows or other physical assaults with weapons, poisons, or whatnot, or from the destruction or theft of one's property, or from deceptions, are not mere conventional injuries. For there are no men, or at least very few, who do not resent actions of this sort. One *learns* to despise the eating of pork, the desecration of a flag, the practice of polygamy, but no instruction or conditioning by society is needed to render a man resentful of a threat to his life or limb. Such resentment results simply from his nature as a man. The same may be said of his resentment of the seizure by stealth or the destruction by violence of things he has come to regard as his own, and of deceptions practiced upon him with the view to exploiting and taking advantage of him. Men everywhere resent actions like these, and not because they have been taught to, or so conditioned by their tribes, but just because they are men.

Property injuries   It might be thought that damage to property, in contrast to damage to one's person, cannot be considered natural injury for the fairly obvious reason that the very concept of property is conventional. *Possession,* to be sure, is no conventional concept, inasmuch as it means simply the having of something within one's power (Lat. *possidere*)—that is, the physical occupancy or grasp of something, together with the ability to hold it. No man-made rules or conventions are needed to determine whether a man does, for example, thus possess a field or building. This can be decided only by trying to dislodge him. But that such a field, building, or anything else should be a man's *property* cannot thus be determined, for the concept of property or ownership is entirely the creation of rules. A man may own a field or building he does not possess, or may similarly possess something he does not really own. One owns something to which he has a valid title, or which he can in other ways declare to be his, by virtue of and in entire dependence upon certain rules and customs.

Can we, then, regard a violation of one's property as a natural and not merely a conventional injury? The answer appears to be that while ownership is the creation of convention, resentment arising from the violation of it is not. That a given building is my property is a fact of convention, a relationship that is entirely the creation of men; but that I should feel injured by someone's destruction of what is thus artificially created is in no similar way conventional. I may learn what, by rule and convention, may be thought of as mine, but I do not similarly learn how to react to its despoilment by others. Or to cite an analogy: The bond of marriage is entirely the creation of custom and law, though it may be based upon needs and desires that are not merely conventional. Thus, to affirm of a certain person that that person is my wife is to affirm the existence of a relationship that is the creation of custom or rule. But it is no mere convention that I should feel resentment if that person is assaulted. Such resentment is not something that is learned, is not something governed by rules, in the sense that it would not exist if it were not for such rules. The rules create the relationship, but not the sense of injury that can arise from it.

In the light of this we can say that while some facts and relationships are the creations of conventions and rules, not all the feelings associated with such facts and relationships are themselves conventional. Some, at least, have their foundation in human nature itself.

Conventional injuries not crimes   This seems to afford the answer to the question that has been raised—the question, namely, of what kind of injury may properly be prohibited by society through the coercion of law. *Any natural injury may thus be prohibited, but merely conventional injuries may not.* This rule is simple in its formulation, but the consequences of applying it would be momentous indeed.

A man may properly and by all means be prevented from assaulting, stealing from, or defrauding another, for the injuries of such actions are natural ones, and the resentment of such injuries natural resentment— not reactions that are learned and thus susceptible to becoming unlearned. No man, on the other hand, may be properly restrained from living in whatever manner he chooses, doing with himself (or with his mind or body) what he will, speaking as he pleases so long as his speech is no part of a fraud upon others, doing as he pleases with whatever is his own, short of using it (e.g., a gun) to inflict injury upon others even though this may, as in the case of a flag or religious artifact, be symbolic of values that are profoundly cherished by others.

No man can assault, steal from, or defraud himself; and accordingly, there can be no natural injury to oneself for which any protection of law is needed. If a normal man injures himself—as, for example, by taking poison or wounding himself inadvertently or carelessly—then he is in the same position as one to whom has befallen a natural evil or catastrophe, like someone who has been struck by a falling boulder. Such possibilities of self-injury call for no curtailment of a man's freedom, any more than does the possibility of ordinary mishap.

If a man injures another but the injury is not a natural one (of the kind just described), then he does, indeed, injure him. A merely conventional injury is no less an injury than a natural one, and sometimes no less injurious, or even far more so. But if *every* injury, including every conventional one, were a fit object of legal prohibition, then there would be no course of conduct that might not quite legitimately be outlawed. For authority to restrain a man in his actions, it would be sufficient that someone complain about them; and since anything whatever is a perfectly appropriate object of resentment and complaint by someone, then anything whatever could be properly forbidden.

But this is not the whole of the answer, for one might take just that position. That is, it might be maintained, and indeed often has been, that no man has any right to do anything except what his society more or less generously permits. It would, for example, be perfectly intelligible that in a given society no man could do anything at all to which any man whatsoever raised even the slightest objection; that a sufficient basis for restraint would be the simple objection on the part of another. In such a society there would, to be sure, be no freedom at all, or at least the very minimum, but it would nevertheless have one genuine advantage—the possibility of injury of any kind by others would be reduced to the absolute minimum.

Injury and the balancing of evils The rest of the answer, then, appears to be this: That while a conventional injury is indeed an injury, and therefore something that, abstractly considered, ought not to be inflicted, the evil of such injury can rarely equal that of its prohibition. Such injury (like any other) can be prevented only by placing restraints upon someone's conduct.

Now we have already noted that, the fulfillment of aim or desire being an absolute good, then freedom, with respect to such fulfillment, is an unqualified good. This does not mean that it may never be curtailed, but only that its curtailment must absolutely be justified in terms of the greater evil of the injury resulting from its exercise. Put more tersely, we can say that restraint is always an evil by its nature, but it is sometimes less so than indulgence.

What has been learned can be unlearned. No man, therefore, should be permitted to appeal to a merely learned and conditioned reaction to another's behavior as a basis for curtailing it. We cannot expect men to learn not to resent assault, theft, and fraud, for such resentment was never learned to begin with, and is thus not susceptible to being unlearned. We can, however, expect men to learn not to resent mere conventional offenses, for such resentment has been learned, exists only because it was learned, and can hence be unlearned. Better, therefore, that men should be permitted to burn flags, revile religion, use strong liquors and drugs, indulge in deviant sexual behavior, and all such things, even at the price of evoking deep resentment and thus real injury in their fellows—better all this than that such actions should be curtailed by the coercion of law. It is better because we can at least hope that such learned resentments are not invincible, that they can at least be overcome. Freedom being unqualifiedly good, its abolishment is unqualifiedly evil; and such abolishment cannot ever be justified except in terms of an even greater evil resulting from its exercise.

Applications Mill concluded his essay with a section entitled "Applications," offering a preview of the new age of liberty that would be ushered in when legislators, magistrates, and mankind generally had grasped and begun to apply his grand principle. We need not follow Mill's example with any similar pleas, but it will be worthwhile to indicate in a general way the consequences of applying the principle that has been enunciated.

Victimless offences Criminologists have lately been propounding the principle that there can be no crime without a victim. In the light of this they have been opposing the practice, particularly prevalent in America, of trying to "legislate morals." Actions which, according to this view, should not be treated judicially as crimes or legal offenses of any kind include such things as drunkenness, obscenity, homosexuality, and so on. Partly their motivation has been, like Mill's, a simple concern for human freedom, but they have also been motivated by considerations of economy. A vast amount of the resources of the police and the entire judicial system is consumed in the attempted suppression of what should be considered, from the standpoint of law (if not from the standpoint of morality), innocent activity.

One can hardly fail to recognize that this formula, "there is no crime where there is no victim," expresses an obvious truth and is indeed hardly more than the expression of common sense. A philosopher is likely to recognize in the term "victim," however, the same fatal ambiguity that was involved in Mill's term "injury." Just what is it to be the "victim" of another man's action? Obviously, it is to suffer *injury* by that man. But here we have to insist that the patriot who sees the flag of his country desecrated by persons he can only regard as cowards is in the fullest sense *injured.* That it does not hurt *him* to see this done is simply untrue. It does not wound his body, but the wound is no less painful for that.

It is hoped that the modification and elaboration of Mill's principle, involving the qualifications of natural and conventional wrong, have removed this difficulty. If so, then the actual workings of that principle are almost too obvious to belabor. We need only to consider a bare sketch of its applications, which will be enough to show that it holds up at those points where Mill's principle, together with certain contemporary formulations from the area of criminology, does not.

Sexual behavior and criminality   One of the more obvious consequences of our principle is that society may not properly interfere with any sexual practices whatever involving adults, except in cases of assault (e.g., rape) or fraud (e.g., seduction of the young). Similarly, the traditional institution of lifelong monogamous marriage, however good, inspiring, and desirable, deserves no protection of law, nor has the state, for that matter, any business meddling in this relationship at all, except indirectly where the safety of children is involved and where the protection of society against contagious disease is implicated. No civil authority may presume to insist upon anyone obtaining its *permission* either for the creation or for the dissolution of this relationship, nor may the state set forth conditions for entering into it or leaving it, except, again, in those rare cases where public safety may be involved or the safety of children somehow jeopardized. Whether a man has one wife, two, or whatever number he may choose; whether a woman has a plurality of spouses to whom she is formally ("legally") married—these things are no business whatever of any legislator. Such matters are fit subjects for guidance and remonstrance from the church (in the case of those who adhere to any church), but not for the compulsive coercion of the secular state. Similarly, it is no business of any magistrate whether anyone has any spouse at all, or if so, for how long, and under what terms or arrangements, nor is it a concern of his whether anyone chooses to cohabit with others of the same or different sex. These things are all matters of convention, posing threat of injury to no one, or at least, to no one except free agents.

Eccentricity and criminal behavior   Again, the life-styles one chooses, his manners, his appearance, his personal preferences and practices, what he does with his time, and whether he uses his resources well or ill—all such matters are clearly beyond the proper concern of any lawmaker. What one does with his own body and mind, whether he uses drugs, intoxicants, poisons, stimulants, or whatnot, whether he engages in activities dangerous to his own well-being, whether he takes certain obvious precautions for his own safety, such as wearing certain safety devices on the public highways or locking up his belongings, are beyond any concern of any legislator. Failure to abide by certain standards in all such things involves danger, to be sure, but it is a danger only to oneself, and only indirectly and remotely to others; and any man has an absolute right to court danger, assuming he knows the nature and degree of his risks. So long as his activity poses no clear threat to others of assault, fraud, or theft, then it is wanton meddling for the state to restrain it or to send police officers against those caught up in it.

It is one thing to point out, however wisely, however incontestably, that a certain type of behavior poses dangers to the agent. It is quite another thing to impose criminal liability upon one for pursuing such activity, in full knowledge of the personal danger to himself. Thus, if a man should wish to experiment with dangerous drugs, then this is a proper occasion to educate him to their danger. It is not an occasion for waiting until he does experiment with them and then arresting him. If someone wishes to get from place to place by soliciting rides from passing motorists, and if such motorists wish to pick up such strangers, knowing the occasional danger of such accommodation, then it is appropriate to publicize the facts and perhaps post reminders of them along the highway. It is not appropriate—and is a serious invasion of liberty—to penalize either those who solicit or those who provide such rides. No driver is obligated to pick up hitchhikers. The choice is his. And the danger, to the rather small extent that it exists at all, is his too.

The principle of criminal legislation   In general, then, a legislator may ask concerning any practice whatever: *Not* whether it is in keeping with morality; *not* whether it accords with the ordinary standards of decency; *not* whether it reflects civilized manners; *not* whether it is offensive to the sensibilities of law-abiding citizens; *not* whether it clashes with the cultural and religious heritage of his society; *not* whether it is perhaps pointless, foolish, and profitless; *not* whether it is in keeping with the minimum standards of personal conduct; and *not* (even) whether it is perhaps extremely dangerous (to him, alone, who undertakes it). Such questions as these are perfectly appropriate for moralists bent upon improving men's characters and perhaps even raising the general level of civilized life, for clergymen concerned with men's salvation, for parents and teachers concerned with the well-being of children, and no doubt for others. They are of no legitimate concern whatever for any lawmaker.

Concerning any practice the lawmaker may ask only: Is it injurious to anyone but the agent? And if he is able to answer "yes" to that question, then he needs to ask still another: Is the injury thus wrought of a kind that would be felt by all or most men, independently of their training, customs, and conventions? And only if *that* question, which is a question of sociology rather than one of jurisprudence, can yield no answer but "yes" does the lawmaker have any concern with the practice at all. The morality of citizens, whether what they are doing is right or wrong, or whether they even know the difference between right and wrong, is of no more concern to him than to any ignorant and idle meddler. The liberty of citizens—and in particular their freedom from pointless and coercive meddling by the agents of the state—is on the other hand a thing of overwhelming importance to those whose freedom the state can almost whimsically jeopardize. Liberty, if not an absolute good, is at any rate an unqualified one, quite regardless of how this or that person may feel about its mode of expression.

Political Obligation   XI

All obligation arises from certain relationships and the rules governing them and evaporates with the absence of either. Like the rules themselves, therefore, obligations are the creations of men and arise from arrangements entered into by men. There is no abstract *moral* obligation that one discovers by studying the heavens or by searching out its eternal law implanted within him. It is rather that some obligations are more important than others, and thus more deserving of honor, for reasons which we shall make clear.

Relationships one source of obligation First of all, a relationship to others is required in order for any obligations to arise. Thus a man without children could have no paternal obligations, one without any faith or church could have no religious obligations, and one belonging to no brotherhood, natural or man-made, could have no fraternal obligations. Contemporary men living in civilized communities have a whole complex web of obligations—to family, employer, church, to each and every voluntary association, and of course to the state itself, all of these involving certain fairly clear and definable relationships to others. Abolish those relationships, and one abolishes the obligations to which they give rise.

Rules the other source More is needed than this, however, to create obligation of any kind. No relationship between persons, just by itself, imposes any obligation upon anyone until that relationship is defined by rules. Thus two men, encountering each other for the first time in some forsaken and desolate place beyond any political jurisdiction, and thus beyond the reach of law or common custom, would have no obligation to each other whatsoever, not even that of respecting life. Their relationship, as far as any obligation is concerned, would not differ from that between a man and a squirrel or a woodchuck. Of course, there might be reasons why each should, for example, keep peace with the other or, beyond that, assist him, if needed, but the reason for this could not be an obligation to. Such men, bringing to this place habits and expectations nourished by civilized life, might retain vestiges of them, in which case certain familiar rules might readily be carried over here. With them would be brought the obligations that such rules define. Rules do not create themselves, however, nor are they given to men by God; and without them no obligations exist.

The other condition necessary for the emergence of an obligation is, accordingly, a rule. In the absence of either—of the relationship between persons, and of a rule or rules defining certain features of that relationship—there is no obligation of any person to any other. But when both of these are given—the relationship and the rule—the obligation is given too.

Thus, returning to that desolate place referred to a moment ago, beyond the reach of rule or law, we can suppose that there was at first only one man there. Clearly, this man would have no *obligation* to someone not even there. Nor has he any obligations to himself. Reasons might be given why he should do some things and avoid doing others, but among those reasons cannot be any statements of his obligations.

But now suppose a second person is introduced into the situation, and the two suddenly confront each other. Has not each the obligation, say, to respect the life and integrity of the other, to leave him unharmed? Hardly. This might express how one or the other, or even both, feel concerning what is appropriate to the situation, but it expresses no obligation. In the absence of any hint of assurance that the other does not in fact intend him great harm, each must keep his guard and his defense. It cannot possibly be an obligation of one to cast aside his weapon and place himself in peril of his very life, having for his security only the wish or the hope that the other shares that sentiment.

Now let us suppose, however, that one of these two extends his open hand, signifying the absence of any offensive intention, and suppose it is seized by the other in recognition of its meaning. At this point a rule emerges, and with it an obligation. Neither may now innocently inflict harm on the other. That is what the gesture means. Until that rule emerges—establishing, incidentally, the barest beginning of a political life—there is no more obligation on the part of anyone than there would be if one of them suddenly confronted, not a man, but an irrational animal or even an inanimate thing.

The indispensability of rules   It is a fond and popular notion that relationships by themselves impose obligations and that the rules are the product of such obligations, rather than the other way around. Thus, it is not hard to believe that a father has certain obligations to his children just because they are his children, quite regardless of whether he recognizes or would respect any rules in which those obligations would be defined.

This is a very suitable kind of relationship by which to test that thesis, for the relationship of father to child is clearly biological and natural, unlike that of husband to wife, which is man-made. A man is the father of a given child because he sired him. Nothing more is required for the existence of the *de facto* relationship. Does that fact, then, give rise to any obligation—for example, the obligation to nourish or protect?

It does not at all. We, knowing what relationship exists, may thoroughly approve of the father's nourishing and protecting; or, in the light of his failure to do so, we may condemn him, and in either case express those sentiments in the language of moral obligation. But no such obligation exists except as imported to the relationship by rules we are in the habit of honoring. Suppose he belongs to a culture in which children are, by rule and long tradition, nourished and raised by their grandparents. Shall we say he has a mistaken or distorted notion of his true obligations? Or suppose this father has sired an idiot. Suppose further that he has inherited a tradition, very remote from ours, in which the rule is conscientiously honored that an idiot child is destroyed as soon as its idiocy is discovered. Now at this point if we feel inclined to say that this man is, after all, the child's father, that he brought it into the world, that he ought therefore to nourish and protect it regardless, that it would be "murder" for him to destroy it, then it is clear that we are invoking all sorts of rules which, man-made though they are, have become part of our cultural conditioning to the point that we imagine we are enunciating obligations woven into the fabric of nature herself. What we are doing is appealing to rules, and *not* just to the existence of a relationship describable in purely biological terms. We are packing into that relationship more than is put there by biology. We are packing into it the very rules we associate with the *social* relationship of fatherhood in our culture, and then imagining that the biological relationship has by itself created the obligations that are derived from the rules that define that relationship. Of course, it may (or it may not) be the case that our rules, defining the obligations of fatherhood, are for certain reasons superior to those that might conflict with them, but this is not to the point.

The irrelevancy of feeling   Two other points must be made before turning to the critical question of political obligation, and those are: first, that an obligation need not be *felt* in order to obtain; and second, that one need not have been an author of the rule creating an obligation in order to be bound by it.

Thus, with respect to the first point, a citizen is obligated to file an income-tax return by a certain date, for example—an obligation that arises from his role as a citizen together with a rule, in this case a law. That these may create in him no sense of obligation, or that he would perhaps feel no guilt in defaulting, does not modify the actual obligation in the least. Indeed, he might for various reasons feel the strongest *moral* obligation not to pay his taxes from considerations of the use to which his taxes are likely to be put; and although this would create at least the appearance of conflict between his political and his moral obligation, it has not the least tendency to erase the former. That someone may be obligated is one thing; that he also feels that obligation is another thing altogether; and although the two often correspond, they do not have to. Neither is a condition of the other. Obligation, and particularly political obligation. would be a strange thing indeed if it arose and fell with one's feelings, obtaining at one moment, vanishing the next, perhaps to reappear a moment later. Laws, moreover, which are the expression of political obligations, would be to no purpose if their force depended upon how this or that citizen felt about them; for to say that one is bound only by such laws as he happens from time to time to feel bound by is about the same as saying that he is bound by no laws at all.

Not all obligation self-imposed   With respect to the second point, it is no condition of an obligation, of whatever sort, that he who is obligated shall have had any hand in the creation of the rule defining it, or even that he should have at one point or another tacitly or otherwise accepted such a rule as applying to him. The opposite supposition, that at least all *political* obligation must in some sense be voluntarily assumed, expresses nothing but a presupposition of certain classical political philosophers that arose from the special circumstances in which they found themselves, having been invented by them as a counterbalance to the claims of kings.

Of course the clearest cases of obligation are voluntary acceptances. Thus, a man binds himself by a promise, a contract, an oath, or a vow, and in such cases there can seldom be any question whether he is bound —he took the obligation upon himself. It is perhaps for this reason that the more important obligations are preceded by the administration of an oath or the declaration of a vow, as in the cases of important public office, the priesthood, certain professions, marriage, and so on. In such cases the person assuming such a role appears to take upon himself its responsibilities. Having thus bound himself, there can be no question that he is obligated, whereas had someone else simply imposed the role upon him, he could have claimed compulsion.

It is with this model in mind that political philosophers have often supposed that the rules governing one's political relationships—that is, the laws of a state—must be the creations of those governed by them (or at least voluntarily accepted by them) if they are to create in them any obligation to obey. It is astonishing the lengths to which men will go in order to render plausible this strange conception. Hardly one person in a thousand has even the least hand in the creation of law, and yet it is pretended that he does, at least in the democratic state, by saying that he makes laws through the agency of his representative in a legislature. Of course he in fact does no such thing; he is more likely than not wholly unknown by that lawmaker and rarely knows from day to day what laws are being created for him or even, fairly often, who is creating them. But because it is thought somehow essential to the validity of a law that it represent the voluntary acceptance of an obligation by whoever is governed by it, the myth is perpetuated that a law's validity is not seriously compromised through the system of representation. And furthermore, those states that lack this arrangement for the creation of law are often portrayed, even by sophisticated political philosophers, as lacking legitimacy. Their laws, it is said, impose no obligations but only threats—just because those to whom they are directed neither made nor voluntarily accepted them. These laws therefore express nothing but the arbitrary rule of a despot.

A man being led to the gas chamber does not imagine that he is the author of the law under which he is now executed, even in the most attenuated sense. The most that can be claimed is that he knew there was such a law, or at least, should have. This has nothing whatever to do with who made it. The laws under which we pay taxes were not made by us, except in the relatively rare cases of referendum; and even here it can hardly be pretended that the minority who voted against those laws were nevertheless somehow their authors. It is the same with all laws. We learn what our political obligations are—that is, what laws we must live by—in the same way that we learn of the laws of some remote jurisdiction in which we have no part, namely, by reading or by consulting an expert. It is not necessary for us to know who made them or how they came to be laws, much less is it necessary for us to imagine that we made them ourselves, or were somehow involved in their creation, or consulted about them. There may be all sorts of reasons for preferring one method of lawmaking to another, for recommending that laws be created by an elected assembly, for example, rather than by some army commander who has taken upon himself the role of chief of state; but the reason cannot be that in the one case laws create political obligations, whereas in the other they do not. They do in both cases.

Most of the rules defining men's obligations, whether moral, political, religious, or whatever, are of ancient origin; and not only did those bound by them have nothing to do with creating them, they do not even know who did. Many laws have their roots in custom, some in religion, and many retain their force long after the passing of whatever gave rise to them. Who of us, for example, invented the rule that one may have only one husband or wife at a time? Who of us was consulted? When were we asked to signify our acceptance of it? There are some who feel no obligation to comply with it, but there it is, all the same, now for good or ill embodied in the law of the state. The *origin* of the rule is irrelevant. Only the fact of it, together with certain relationships, is needed in order to impose obligation.

What political obligation is   A political obligation, therefore, is a duty defined by the law of the state. The two conditions necessary for the creation of obligation are present—namely, certain relationships and certain rules. The relationships are all those by which a given people constitute a nation, and the rules are the laws of that state. Whatever is required by law is a political obligation, and nothing is a political obligation unless it is required by law. The laws define one's obligations as a member of that body politic. They do no more. They do not express his moral obligations nor his religious obligations, unless accidentally they happen to enjoin certain actions that his morality or his religion also require. But they do answer, and answer completely, the question: What are my obligations as a member of this state? To know his political obligations a citizen needs only to know what is required by law. He need not ascertain how he feels about this or that law, nor how it came to be law.

All political obligations, although they are defined by the law of the state, are improperly represented as obligations *to* the state. *Some* are—our obligations to pay taxes, for example. These are paid to the state. But laws requiring us to respect the property of our neighbor define obligations to our neighbor, not to the state. It is the same with respect to most laws. Political obligations, like all others, arise from certain relationships, but the relationships of a political community are far more complex than the single one of ruler and ruled. Virtually all of the criminal law sets limits to one's conduct with respect not simply to those who govern, but with respect to everyone. In being forbidden by law to defraud, I am not merely forbidden to defraud the state, but to defraud anyone; and while a highway patrolman is an agent of the state who enforces its laws and thus the obligations of those who live under them, it is only seldom that he is enforcing any obligation to the state itself. In obeying him, one is not normally "rendering unto Caesar" (that is, to the state) anything at all. One is instead rendering unto his fellow men what is, by law, due them.

The Defeasibility of Political Obligations

Under what conditions, then, does a law of the state fail to impose obligation? The answer to this is, roughly: When it is useless. There is a tendency to think of obligations as independent of practical concerns, and then to imagine that some of them—moral ones, for example, or duties to God—have somehow a stronger claim than one's political duties. Sometimes they do, but not just because they are of a moral or religious character. It is, rather, that more is at stake in these cases, and the obligations they supersede are thus relatively worthless. We shall now try to make this clear.

Human relationships are governed by rules, some of great importance, some less so. People cannot even enter into a game of tiddlywinks without rules, nor into any intercourse whatsoever other than belligerence and warfare. Such rules, then, have a practical foundation. Generally speaking, they enable the participants in the relationship, whatever it is, to achieve the broad goals that give it meaning to begin with. Thus if a club is formed with the purpose, let us suppose, of fostering an interest in bird-watching, or in sailing, or whatever, then the rules that will govern the particular relationships of its members will be those that are effective to this end, and they will define the obligations of the club members, obligations not shared by those who are not members. If it were then discovered, however, that some such obligation conflicted with another—with the law of the state, for example—then one obligation would have to yield to another. The way to express this, however, is to say that two rules conflict, not that one or the other was never a rule in the first place.

The analogy of a state to a club is of course imperfect, but a state is nevertheless, like a club, a man-made thing, and its rules also have purposes that enable men to achieve those ends for which they have created a political life. Such rules—that is, laws—therefore define obligations for the members of that state, which is to say, they define their political obligations. The laws may sometimes be bad, wicked, or unjust. This does not alter their status as laws, nor does it remove the political obligations they impose. One may thus sometimes have a political obligation to do what is wicked or unjust. But is that the last word on the subject? Hardly—except in the case of a man, if there is any such, who recognizes no obligations higher than those imposed by a state, i.e., by a political law-maker.

We confront the question, then: Under what conditions may one disregard the law of the state?

One should not say: When the law is unjust, and therefore not a law in the first place. It is not required that any law meet this or that moralist's standard of justice in order to have the force of law. A law is not to be disregarded just because it seems to this or that man to be "unjust." The two conditions of obligation are a certain relationship and a rule; it does not have a third condition—that one bound by this rule should *feel* obligated by it, nor do any feelings he has enter into the picture at all.

Again, one should not say that a law may be disregarded when it violates one's conscience, and for the same reason. Laws, to be laws, are not required to meet the varying tests of conscience of those to whom they are meant to apply; they do not cease to be laws the moment they are confronted by someone who dislikes them.

And yet there are sometimes reasons for disregarding the law of the state and refusing, as it is rhetorically expressed, to render unto Caesar what belongs to God. This slogan, like the shibboleths just considered, is an inept way of expressing what is sometimes true.

Three grounds for disobedience   There appear to be three quite different grounds upon which a law may properly be disregarded and a political obligation thus ignored. The first two are cases in which a political obligation is practically nullified by certain considerations, and the third, that in which a political obligation is overturned by a "higher" one.

The first is when the purpose of the law, though valuable in itself, is in no way achieved by compliance *in a given instance,* and may even be defeated by compliance.

The second is when the general purpose of the law, though worthy in itself, is not achieved by compliance *in any instance.*

And the third is when the purpose achieved by compliance, though worthwhile, is of *more limited significance* than one achieved by compliance with another rule that conflicts with the law.

It is this last, involving what is usually called a conflict of obligations, that generates the deeper passions and sometimes the impulse to martyrdom or rebellion. We shall illustrate all three.

Every rule that creates an obligation has some purpose; or if it has not, then it is frivolous and not worth discussing, for the obligation it gives rise to is as pointless as the rule itself and may be disregarded at will. Those rules which are the laws of the state, then, have purposes. They were not enacted whimsically nor arbitrarily. They have a point. The point or purpose may not in every case be important, but it is there, or at least it was once. Whether there is some ultimate purpose to all legislation such as the common good, human happiness, or whatnot, is a question we need not consider here.

Cases of pointless compliance   What, then, if compliance with the law defeats the very purpose of the law? Consider the following trivial example. The law requires one to stop before a red traffic light. Suppose, then, that on an empty highway, in the middle of night, one is on an urgent mission—perhaps rushing someone suddenly stricken to a hospital —and is confronted by a red light. Does he have an obligation to stop? Yes—the circumstances here do not nullify the law in question, and that law creates a political obligation. Should he stop? No—for the very purpose served by the law, and hence the basis for the obligation itself— public safety—is *not* served in this instance, and is in fact defeated. The temptation here is to say that the law of the state—a traffic ordinance in this case—conflicts with a higher law of moral obligation, but this need not be so in the least. One may have no obligation whatever of any kind to serve the stricken person in the manner suggested, but only, perhaps, a strong wish to. The conflict is, rather, a pragmatic one—between the purpose of the law itself and the effect of observing it in this instance. The obligation is nullified by the very purpose of the law which gave rise to it in the first place.

Frivolous law   In the second type of case, an obligation is nullified, not by the fact that compliance would be pointless in a given case, but by the fact that it would be generally pointless. This is the case of the frivolous or ill-conceived law that often results from ignorance on the part of the lawmaker.

For example, in pursuit of public health and safety, it is enacted that no one may use certain substances believed to be dangerous, and their sale, possession, or use are declared to be felonies under the criminal law. But suppose that in point of fact those substances are not dangerous in any of the respects imagined by the legislator, or are in any case less so than various other things in common use. This kind of case differs from the one just considered in this respect: that while one should heed traffic regulations and disregard them in good conscience only in special circumstances, one should in general disregard regulations of this sort. There is in both cases a law and, hence, a political obligation. One would in either case be subject to arrest and, at the level of legality, properly so. In the first case that obligation is overridden by the pointlessness of the rule in a particular instance. In the second case it is overridden by the general pointlessness of the rule.

Conflicts of obligations   By far the more significant conflict, however, is the third kind—between a political obligation and one that is thought to be higher or more compelling, such as a moral or religious obligation. Such cases arise, and sometimes very painfully, when one is called upon by the state to an obligation which is in clear conflict with his religion, to violate the sabbath, for example, or is summoned to bear arms, in conflict with conscience and certain deep convictions concerning the sanctity of human life. Here the temptation is almost overwhelming to say that the law of the state imposes no real obligation, or is perhaps not even a law, or that one can never really be obligated to do anything in violation of his holy religion, or his conscience, or his deeply held moral convictions, and so on.

Of course the difficulty with such protestations is that they are too vague and sometimes confused. One recognizes a certain truth in them, yet it is difficult to say just what that truth might be.

Let us consider some examples of such conflict, some fairly trivial and others involving larger issues. Formally, the examples will be all alike, each involving conflict between a political obligation and another that is deemed "higher," i.e., a religious or moral obligation. The thing then to note is that while they are formally the same, they are not resolved the same way, and having seen that, we can then see just what substantive consideration is at work in our resolution of them.

Consider, then, these cases:

1. *The law of the state requires that slow-moving vehicles display large colorful emblems to warn other vehicles and thus reduce the likelihood of collision. Members of a religious sect who are forbidden to use motor vehicles and who therefore use horses and wagons on the highway, refuse to comply, citing the prohibition in their religion of ornamentation and ostentatious display. They say they will render unto Caesar only that which is Caesar's, but unto God that which is His.*

2. *The state requires the education of all children to age sixteen. The members of a religious sect refuse to comply; they declare that this*

would lead their children to worldliness and jeopardize their chance of salvation. They say they will obey God before man.

3. *The law of the state requires all school exercises to begin with certain observances, among them a pledge of allegiance to the state itself. Members of a religious group instruct their children not to comply, insisting that their only allegiance is to God.*

4. *A community is threatened with an epidemic. The Department of Public Health is authorized, under such circumstances, to vaccinate everyone considered vulnerable to the infection. Certain citizens refuse vaccination for themselves and their children, citing the words of the Bible, and in particular James 5:15: "And the prayer of faith shall save the sick, and the Lord shall raise him up." The maladies of the body, they say, are healed by faith alone.*

5. *The law of the state prohibits homicide, including the willful destruction of children. Certain otherwise law-abiding citizens refuse to comply, pointing out that their religion requires periodic human sacrifice on certain solemn occasions, and in particular requires the destruction of children chosen by lot.*

6. *The law requires that male citizens of certain qualifications and age register for military service. Some citizens refuse, pointing out that they were born into a religious tradition that has always prohibited bearing arms under any circumstances.*

7. *With respect to the same law, other citizens take the position that, while they have no religious scruple against bearing arms, it violates their conscience, and for this reason they refuse to comply.*

8. *With respect to the same law, still other citizens take the position that, while they have no religion at all and are not guided in matters of morality by any supposed conscience, they nevertheless refuse to comply on philosophical grounds—namely, that they cherish human life and certain human rights, and that under the circumstances they would be lending their support to policies enormously destructive of these with no hope of achieving objectives commensurate with such destruction.*

These cases are quite varied, and each presents a conflict between an actual political obligation and an obligation of another kind, generally deemed "higher."

With respect to them, we wish to show, *first,* that there is no single answer to the question of which obligation should prevail; *second,* that when circumstances are made sufficiently full and clear, it is possible to resolve the conflict in each case, usually with confidence; and *third,* that there is a guiding principle at work in yielding those resolutions. Once that guiding principle is made known, then, we are in a position to answer the general question of when a political obligation is overturned by another, and when it is not.

The danger of formalism   Meanwhile something should be said of the danger and futility of seeking a purely formal solution to this question—

that is, of trying to show that obligations of a given *kind* must always be honored over those of another kind. It is a misrepresentation, and a dangerous one, to affirm that religious duties take precedence over secular ones, that the will of God must be heeded rather than the will of men, that no law should be permitted to prevail against the obligations imposed by the moral law, that one should render unto Caesar only that which is not due to God, and so on. The danger of every such position is this: That having taken that position with respect to a given conflict of obligations, it is usually possible for someone trying to undermine it to present another, perhaps imaginary, specimen of such conflict, formally identical with the one in question, but concerning which the same position is enormously difficult to maintain. The defender of that position then finds that he either must stick to it, however implausibly, with respect to the new case, or else admit that his original position was not without exceptions. Many conscientious objectors to war have found themselves squirming on the horns of this dilemma. For example, having taken the view that violence is *always* to be rejected on the ground that the moral obligation to respect human life prevails over every possible consideration to the contrary, they then find themselves asked to state their reactions to various imagined situations involving rapists, madmen, virgin sisters, sinking lifeboats, and so on. In such cases the formal answer that a certain kind of obligation, *as such,* must always be respected over all others is far less plausible and, in fact, sometimes absurd. Therefore, the conscientious objector must bravely "stick to his guns," asserting the absurd time after time, perceiving that the moment he admits an exception he has lost his case, or in other words, has formally abandoned his own position. It is an exceptionally bad way to resolve a problem of obligation, for it not only produces hypocrites and fools but, worse, obscures important problems that could be made clear.

Thus, consider the first case, involving garish emblems to warn vehicles approaching from the rear. Suppose (a) it is discovered that over the course of years there have been many collisions with the wagons driven by members of this sect, that they are increasing as traffic increases, with frequent death and injury resulting, that they seem to be due largely to the fact that oncoming vehicles do not see the wagons in time to avoid them, and that methods of reducing this danger, without the use of such emblems, offer little hope of success.

Or (b) suppose on the contrary it is discovered that members of this sect always drive their wagons in the early morning hours when there is little traffic, that they customarily drive them out of the line of traffic as much as possible, and that in fact there has never been a single collision with one of them.

Clearly the issue has nothing to do with religion, the will of God, or whatnot. Without for a moment presuming to speak on any question of theology, it can be said, in case the truth is expressed by (b), that the law should simply make an exception for vehicles driven in the manner described, thus *eliminating* the conflict. This would, on the other hand, seem absurd if the truth is expressed by (a). Here it at least makes sense to say that the political obligation should prevail, or else that such wagons should be kept from the highway altogether.

But what has happened here? Note that the problem has ceased to be one of balancing obligations in the abstract, but has instead become one of assessing practical consequences.

Case 2, involving enforced schooling, lends itself to similar treatment. Suppose it is found, for example, that the community has never suffered in any demonstrable way as the result of children of this sect abandoning school earlier than others, and that it would in fact be highly disruptive of peace and order to treat the religious scruples of these people, with respect to this question, as crimes. The answer again becomes quite clear, and it has nothing to do with religious or abstract ethics. It has only to do with the practical ends of the law, which is all that justifies political obligation in the first place.

Case 3 is similar, in that the mere refusal of children to participate in ritual—a pledge of allegiance in this case—hardly threatens any purpose for which the criminal law is established. Here we need not attempt to balance a religious obligation against a political one, but only to ask what difference it would make in terms of consequences to the community.

But now consider case 4, involving an epidemic. Suppose (a) that the epidemic in question is one of a very mild influenza, the worst effects of which cause slight fever and discomfort for a day or two. Who is going to say that under these conditions the political obligation must be honored, and everyone vaccinated, perhaps at great cost and discomfort, as well as resentment on the part of persons of this religious persuasion?

Suppose on the other hand (b) that the epidemic is of a particularly virulent and dangerous infection, that those who were not vaccinated in the past, including many children, did almost invariably die as a result, and that there is no other way of meeting such danger. Clearly, the whole problem has shifted; but it is formally *still* the problem of weighing one kind of obligation against another. Actually, however, it is a question of practical consequences.

With case 5, involving human sacrifice, this becomes perfectly evident. Formally, we have here a simple conflict between political and religious obligation, no different from the pledge of allegiance case, yet no one not a member of this sect would imagine that the religious obligation should be given priority. Why not? The answer is too obvious to set down.

And finally, considering cases 6, 7, and 8, we have three different kinds of conflict—that between political obligation and (a) religion, (b) "conscience" or personal ethics, and (c) certain practical considerations.

Strangely and interestingly, the state has traditionally taken the position that only the first of these counts; that is, that only a traditional *and inherited* religious (as opposed to merely moral) scruple is allowable in this matter, which is flatly inconsistent with the weight allowed to other religious scruples. Thus no one considers it a valid defense of the practice of human sacrifice that it is commanded by some traditional and inherited religion. Even the practice of polygamy, relatively harmless though it is, has not been tolerated on that ground, despite the fact that such a ground does provably exist, and that some of the adherents of this religion do most surely believe that it expresses the will of God. So the state is placed in the strange and indefensible position of saying that the obligations imposed by law are necessarily overriden by religious conviction—provided there is a traditional and inherited religious obligation in conflict with them—but that this formal priority of religious over political obligation shall be conclusive in some cases and without any weight at all in others; in other words, there is no such formal priority after all!

How conflicts of obligation are resolved We have seen that, in the last analysis, substantive considerations determine the resolution of such conflicts of obligation in spite of what appears to be a felt need to represent them as purely formal; and the substantive consideration that finally settles things is a consideration of practical consequences. No one would dream of saying that certain persons within the jurisdiction of a contemporary civilized state and subject to its laws must be permitted to practice human sacrifice on the ground that this is a religious duty, enjoined by traditional and inherited religious teaching, and that religious obligations are, after all, of higher authority than any merely political laws. Yet precisely that defense is considered allowable for a conscientious objector to war and was at one time the only defense permitted. The reasoning is, of course, impeccable. If one should obey God before man, then no other conclusion is possible. But behind that reasoning lies the thing that really counts—namely, consideration of the practical consequences of disregarding the law of the state. Strangely enough, however, if a conscientious objector to war takes that very position as his reason for refusing military service, as in our case 8, then he is considered to be on weak and shaky ground! It is precisely the position the state takes, without saying so, when it enjoins the adherents of various religious sects to obey man, in some cases, rather than God.

The obligation to be law-abiding Is there, then, an obligation to obey the law? Or, which is the same question, are there political obligations? Of course there are. There is an obligation to obey each and every rule that applies to a citizen by virtue of his relationship to others, and the laws of the state are such rules, applying to him by virtue of his purely political relationships—that is, those that make him a member of that commonwealth. Some have spoken of some such obligations as being merely *prima facie* ones in view of the fact that they do not always obtain, but this is misleading. It suggests that the laws of the state, for example, impose only *apparent* obligations. The obligations they impose are always real, provided the purposes intended by such rules are in fact served by them. They are, however, sometimes overridden by other obligations whose purposes are of greater significance. They are not, contrary to what men like to imagine, overridden by obligations which are by their nature "higher," being of a religious or moral character. In the case of a conflict of obligations, when every other consideration has failed, and often long before then, the consideration that does finally decide the matter is *not* whether one of the obligations is derived from God, from conscience, or from some supposedly eternal moral law, but simply this one: What practical difference is it going to make?

Some persons feel uncomfortable in reducing all questions of obligation to this, as it seems to place purely practical questions above those of moral or religious duty, but there is no avoiding this. Those who are made uncomfortable about it have, in any case, failed to understand the nature of obligation, of whatever kind, its relationships to rules, and the rationale of rules themselves. Rules, and the obligations they generate, are not kept alive by any kind of energy inherent in themselves. They derive their life and importance from that which gives birth to them in the first place, and that is the practical needs of men living together in some sort of body politic.

Legitimacy XIII

Consider two different ways in which one might be obliged to yield his purse to another. In one case he is ordered by a bandit, brandishing a gun in his face. In the other, a comparable but less crude order is imposed by the tax collector, and like the first, it is accompanied by threats of unpleasant consequences in case of failure to comply.

The two situations are rather similar. In both, one is forced, under threat, to deliver up something that is his. They would normally be distinguished, however, by saying that the tax collector, unlike the bandit, has the *right* to make this demand; that his order, unlike that of the bandit, is a *legitimate* one; or that in the one case something is *owed*, whereas in the other case it simply is *seized*. These are, of course, all just different ways of saying the same thing—of distinguishing between legitimate and illegitimate exercises of power. In both cases one is obliged to yield to superior power, but in the one the power is accompanied by right, whereas in the other it expresses sheer might without right—or at least, so most persons would suppose.

What, then, gives the tax collector this right? What makes his demand, in contrast to that of the bandit, legitimate? Or, broadening the question, under what conditions are the orders imposed by government legitimate? What confers upon some men the right to rule beyond the mere power to compel? Under what conditions is allegiance and obedience owed to a given establishment, rather than being simply enforced?

Most men do not worry unduly about this question. If they awaken some morning to read in the newspaper that their government has been overthrown by a military junta and banished from the land, this news is apt to be received along with the rest as perhaps of greater moment, as perhaps threatening or, conversely, reassuring, but not necessarily as a call to defiance. Most men under such circumstances will go about their day much as they would have otherwise, obeying the police and the laws as before, paying their taxes, and so on. Similarly, but less dramatically, it is not at all uncommon for a man to move his home and family to a new city where his opportunities seem bright, in the full knowledge that this city is governed by a corrupt political machine whose power is held year in and year out by fraud, deception, collusion, and bribe. His relationship to that government thus becomes in all essentials like that to a bandit, lacking every trace of legitimacy, but with this difference: he is likely to have a clearer idea of what will be expected of him in the one case than in the other. He may, in fact, even have reason to believe that he will receive favored treatment from the corrupt political boss, whereas his fate at the hands of the bandit is more problematical.

A philosophical mind finds this intolerable, that a rational man would freely and complacently *place himself* at the mercy of a power that has no semblance of political legitimacy, and that has in fact every sign of being criminal in nature. A government that rules by might only, without right, is no more than a band of criminals. It cannot levy a tax, it can only exact tribute; it cannot fine, it can only extort; and it cannot make law, it can only coerce by threat.

What, then, gives a government this right or legitimacy? What is wanting in the case of a ruling establishment which lacks it? Is it free election? The approval of the church? The wisdom of those who govern? Hereditary title? Subscription to revolutionary doctrine without revision or compromise? A contract with those governed? Or what?

Legitimacy and justification   The first step in answering this question is to distinguish it from another with which it is usually confused—the question of the *justification* of government. It is one thing to ask what, if anything, renders a particular government, or a particular policy or law of that government, or government in general, *legitimate,* and quite another to ask for the *justification* of any of these. Thus a given law may be perfectly legitimate but totally without justification; and similarly, an order may, though justified, be without legitimacy. Suppose, for example, a tax is levied in accordance with the law, and the revenue thus raised foolishly squandered on some vain and frivolous project. The tax is without justification—but this by itself does not cancel its legitimacy or the right to impose it, for the ruling establishment which levied that tax might still be the lawful or *de jure* government, however lacking in wisdom.

Again, suppose there has been a serious traffic accident on a busy through-way, and because of the resulting congestion the ambulance and other emergency vehicles cannot get to it. A police officer, still in uniform, driving home from another jurisdiction and having no authority what-soever in this place, nevertheless takes it upon himself to direct the traffic and clear the congestion, thereby enabling rescue vehicles to ap-proach. His orders are without legitimacy and unlawful, but nonetheless justified by the circumstances.

Implied in these two examples is the basis for distinguishing ques-tions of political legitimacy from those of justification. The former are questions of law, and thus resolved by reference to rules, but the latter are questions of philosophy, and resolved by reference to purposes or ends. The difference is very great, and much political philosophy has been darkened by treating all such questions as if they were the same. In fact it has been typical for political philosophers, seeking a justifica-tion for government, or for some special form of it, to try to prove its legitimacy on the basis of some quasi-legalism such as contract, the will of the governed, or whatnot, and then imagine that they have resolved the problem. Indeed, it is not unknown for such thinkers, after failing to find any such legalism adequate to the purpose, to conclude that govern-ment as such is without justification—and then seriously to suggest its abolishment!

Examples of legitimacy Let us begin, then, with simple cases where legitimacy, or the lack of it, can be established in a simple and straight-forward way.

Case 1.–A farmer makes a number of purchases, then declines to pay the sales tax demanded by the clerk.

Can he do that? May the farmer legitimately refuse to pay the tax for which he is billed? Let us suppose he produces a recent memorandum sent to him from the Department of Agriculture noting that the state legislature has exempted from sales tax all items to be used in agricultural production. He declares that the items in question are to be so used, and files with the vendor a signed exemption certificate to this effect. Our question is now answered: the clerk may not legitimately collect the tax, for no tax exists for these items.

Case 2.–It is discovered that a judge fraudulently misrepresented his qualifications at the time of his appointment by the Governor, having forged various certificates of university degrees and other documents normally considered essential to establish qualification for such office. He has in fact, we may suppose, never formally studied nor practiced law, but simply gleaned what he could of the subject by reading. When this is finally discovered his appointment to the bench is revoked by the Governor, the "judge" is tried for fraud and convicted.

Now the questions arise: Did the man hold office legitimately? And were the decisions he rendered while on the bench legitimate? Must they still be adhered to by the litigants for whom they were rendered? Or were they merely the opinions of a layman, without legal force? A higher court rules on this question to the effect that a man is made a judge, not by his learning but by his appointment by the Governor, that the judge in question did hold office by such appointment, and his rulings are therefore still binding in law.

Case 3.—Let us imagine a small and backward nation which has, as far back as its history is recorded, been governed by kings holding hereditary title to rule. The origins of this ruling family are unknown, but some of its earliest members are believed to have been chieftains who gained their ascendency through a series of tribal wars. Eventually this ruling family became complacent, inept, and corrupt, so that the nation sank deeper and deeper into ignorance and poverty. Finally the last of these kings was deposed by a resourceful and idealistic military commander and allowed to live out his days impotently at his family estate, the commander meanwhile taking into his own hands all the powers of government. He fashioned a new constitution that provided for free elections after his own death, built schools and hospitals, encouraged industry and art, established peaceful relations with all neighboring countries, and in the course of time lifted his country from poverty and ignorance so that it became a model of social justice and progress.

What, then, was the legitimate government of that country? On the day prior to the coup the supreme governmental authority resided in the person of the king and nowhere else. The fact that this king was inept and corrupt does not affect the legitimacy of his rule in the slightest; he was, beyond any doubt, the king. It was he who received ambassadors, he who would on that day have appointed and dismissed cabinet ministers, pardoned criminals and commuted death sentences, and exercised any other function belonging to a chief of state. On the day after the coup he might have claimed, with plausibility, that he still represented the *legitimate* (though powerless) government of that nation, that the military commander was a usurper of power and a bandit who had no trace of right or authority to rule, but only the power that is bestowed by gunpowder. Ten years later he might still have made this claim for the very same reasons, pointing out that he alone held the hereditary right to govern, but it would by then have lost its plausibility. And twenty years later, after this king had died and the new constitution been put into effect, his son could make exactly the same claim, but now with no plausibility whatsoever. If this powerless son were, from the remote estate of his family, to claim the right to receive new ambassadors, veto acts of the legislature, appoint and dismiss cabinet ministers, command the armed forces, and so on, basing these claims on the facts of his ancestry, this would everywhere be recognized as no more than an acting out of delusions of grandeur. Yet the claims were made by his father, were then based on exactly the same foundation, which was at one time everywhere accepted as conferring legitimacy. Criticism of the father's rule was at no point directed at his claim to hold power by right, but at its ineptitude and corruption.

The levels of legitimacy   These examples enable us to distinguish three levels of political legitimacy, and in them we can see exactly what, at each level, it consists of. These three levels are (a) the legitimacy of a law, policy, or governmental order, (b) the legitimacy of office, and (c) the legitimacy of a particular government. A fourth level, the legitimacy or *de jure* character of government as such (as distinguished from some particular government), is something fabulous and metaphysical, as we shall see, and has no existence at all outside philosophical speculations.

At the first level, that of particular policies or orders, political legitimacy consists simply of positive legality. Thus, had the farmer declared that he owed no tax because it was prohibited by some principle of his morality or perhaps by the law of God which, as interpreted by him, forbade tribute to any secular power, then *his* so-called law, or that of his religion, would have been without political legitimacy. It might have possessed a personal legitimacy—that is, been in accordance with his own code of morals—or theological legitimacy—in accordance with the law of his church or, for that matter, in accordance with the very will of God. This, however, would have had nothing whatever to do with its political legitimacy, which is what we are considering. Legitimacy at this level is a straightforward question of fact, and has no connection with philosophy, theology, or morals. The question whether a particular policy or order is legitimate is simply the question whether it is in accordance with the law of the state, whatever that might in fact be. Such law need not be good law, or wise, or even moral; it need only be law that exists.

What, then, of particular laws themselves? By virtue of what are these legitimate? Here, significantly, we find that the legitimacy of a law of the state consists simply of its existence, that the customary distinction of *de jure* and *de facto* does not exist at this level. The question of whether such and such is a legitimate law is nothing but the question of whether it is law.

There are not two kinds of law, those that have and those that lack legitimacy, for the latter are not laws to begin with. Of course, even at this level legitimacy can be represented as accordance with law if one distinguishes different levels of law. Thus an ordinance of a village is legitimate if enacted in accordance with procedures described in law; a statute is legitimate if in accordance with the constitution of the state, and so on. If approached in that way, however, it must then be noted that no question of legitimacy can arise concerning the highest law of the state such as the constitution or, in states despotically ruled, the expressed will of the despot. To ask whether such law is legitimate is simply to ask whether it exists; for example, whether there is such a constitution, or an expressed will of a despot, or whatever else might be accepted there as supreme law.

At the second level, that of the legitimacy of political office, we find something very similar: such office, and the power expressed through it, are legitimately held provided they are held in accordance with law. Thus the judge, however fraudulent his claims, did hold office in accordance with law—that is, by appointment of the Governor as provided by law. Perhaps there were thousands of men better qualified for that office, any of whom the Governor would have preferred had he not been deceived, but this makes not the slightest difference as far as the legitimacy of his exercise of political (in this case, judicial) power is concerned.

And finally, at the third level, we find that the legitimacy of a particular government is, up to a point, the same: supreme authority within a state is legitimately held provided it is held in accordance with law. But here a crucial difference emerges as the result of the fact that government is itself the *source* of law. Beyond a certain point, therefore, the legitimacy of a government is simply its existence. At this point there simply is no distinction between *de jure* and *de facto* government, so that to ask whether a given government is the lawful authority with a given body politic is simply to ask whether it is the government, nothing more. The philosophical significance of this point is rather large, if for no other reason than that so much political philosophy has been created in disregard of it. Its practical significance is hardly less, in light of certain accepted practices concerning the "recognition" of some governments by others.

Philosophical implications of this   Most classical political philosophers, for example, and even contemporary ones, have labored with the question of what renders a particular government that does actually govern legitimate, and indeed, with the larger question of what renders government itself such. Usually at the foundation of such philosophy is the unexamined presupposition that government must somehow rest on the consent of the governed if its claim of legitimacy is to be accepted, or even, that its policies must express, from one day to the next, the will of the governed. Or if neither of these, then there must be some sort of agreement or compact between rulers and ruled; otherwise, the former can be accused of ruling by sheer force, and hence illegitimately. The problem becomes very acute when it is seen that in no literal sense does *any* government, including the very best, rule by the *consent* of the governed. At best it can only rule by the consent of the majority of them, and even here the notion of *consent* is severely stretched. Nor does any government actually express the *will* of those governed, or even, literally, the majority of them. At best it is elected by those governed after all sorts of machinations in which "consent' can be discovered only in the most attenuated sense of the term. So the job of political philosophy becomes that of inventing all sorts of fictitious devices to affirm the requisite "consent" or "will of the governed," where in truth it does not exist (thereby giving birth to fabulous theories), or else concluding that *no* government is *or can be* a government *de jure* or legitimate. The truth, however, appears to be the exact opposite: *every* government which is in fact a government is unavoidably a government *de jure,* the distinction between *de jure* and *de facto* evaporating at this level. The expression, *de jure,* it should be remembered, means *by law.* It does not mean "in accordance with the presuppositions of morality" or anything of this sort.

Suppose, in terms of our example, the attempt on the part of the commander to overthrow the established but corrupt government had almost but not quite succeeded, and that the king, at the brink of defeat, had finally rallied sufficient power and support from certain factions of his army to keep the reins of government in his hands. In this case, of course, the daring commander would have been tried for treason and executed as a rebel against the rightful and legitimate authority of the state. And properly so, assuming there was legal provision for the death penalty in cases of treason; for it is no condition of the legitimacy of any government that it be free from corruption or its power exercised in accordance with this or that philosopher's personal notions of justice or virtue. Its necessary condition of legitimacy is that it exist, and that condition is sufficent.

However, in our example, the coup did succeed and the commander seized absolute power by sheer force. Was his rule, then, legitimate? Certainly it was not in accordance with law, for there was nothing in the laws or the traditions of this country that provided for succession by such means as this. Yet in fact his rule *was* legitimate, or rather, it very soon became so. At what point? At precisely the point when it became *in fact* the supreme political power within that body politic. At that point, at the point where this was the government *de facto,* it also became the source of law itself, the government *de jure.*

And such is in fact what the claim of every government on the face of the earth, the best as well as the worst, finally rests upon; namely, on the fact that it governs. No question can arise, once that fact is established, whether it is a *lawful* government, whether its power is legitimately exercised, or whether it has a right to govern. The distinction between a *de facto* and a *de jure* exercise of power can be made only when the latter can be represented as being in accordance with law. It cannot be made with respect to the very *source* of political law. A despot who governs absolutely, whose expressed will has in fact the force of law, cannot possibly govern illegitimately, or without right. His rule may violate this or that person's sense of morality, or the political or ethical standards which this or that man may have come to honor; it may violate this or that man's notion of God's will. It may violate what this or that philosopher believes *should* be the law for every nation; it may in fact violate the commonest standards of wisdom and justice. Further, it may be well worthwhile to point these things out to achieve a moral condemnation of such rule in the minds of one's audience. But what cannot properly be said is that such rule lacks legitimacy. In the realm of political power there is no higher authority than the possession of power itself, for it is only through this that anything becomes law in the first place. To speak, therefore, of such power—the power to make law—as *illegitimately held* and thus not in accordance with law, is to speak in self-contradiction. The author of these remarks can only condemn such power as contrary to his religious sentiments, his moral sentiments, his political sentiments, his philosophical sentiments, his notions of justice, his preference for another regime, or something of this sort. It would thus be better if they were expressed in these straightforward terms rather than creating paradox, confusion, and wasted philosophical discourse by putting them in terms of legitimacy.

The practical significance of this   The most obvious practical consequence of these reflections is that no rebel or revolutionary regime may properly be denied recognition by other nations, provided it does in fact hold political power securely and is known to do so. For any government to say of another that it governs illegitimately, that it is only a *de facto* and not a *de jure* government, is the wildest kind of dishonesty and hypocrisy. The laws, policies, and political offices of no *de facto* government can lack legitimacy, nor can any such government, considered as a source of law, possibly be unlawful. Yet it is, of course, common practice to pretend otherwise. The United States government, for example, refused to "recognize" the *de facto* government of the Soviet Union for about fifteen years, pretending that this nation's despotic ruler, during those years, was not its legitimate ruler. Even more astonishingly, and with incredible hypocrisy and pretense, it has for two decades refused to recognize the government of China as lawful or legitimate, though never doubting that it does in fact govern China. Instead, it pretends that the "real" government of that vast nation exists on the island of Taiwan, even though representatives of that allegedly lawful government would be arrested and probably put to death if they so much as set foot within the country of which they are said to be the true and rightful government. The explanation of such policies is, of course, that political recognition is used as a lever of international politics and is accordingly withheld as a means of exercising power—all this being partly concealed by a contrived legalism. This may or may not be justified, but it is worth pointing out that it is not really honest.

The legitimacy of government as such   What, then, of the legitimacy of government itself? Can this be considered a fourth level? That is, having considered the legitimacy of particular policies and orders, of political offices, and of particular governments, can we now ask what renders government *as such* legitimate? Can we ask by what right *any* men ever govern others?

It is a question that is often raised, but we should now be able to see that it is senseless. It can only begin to make sense when confused with the question of the justification of government, which we have seen is something quite different.

Questions of legitimacy are, strictly speaking, always questions of rules. That is legitimate which is in accordance with rule. The concept is therefore relative, because one and the same thing can be legitimate in relation to one set of rules (e.g., those of a particular state) and not so in relation to another set (e.g., those of a particular church). Now there happen to be rules by which the legitimacy of a particular governmental order can be tested—namely, the law of the state. There are, similarly, rules by which to test the legitimacy of the exercise of political power— namely, the same law. In case the political power in question is the very power to make law, and such power exists in a particular government or, perhaps, in an individual despot, then such power cannot, we have seen, be illegitimately held, though it may be foolishly or even wickedly exercised in relation to someone's conception of folly and wickedness.

What, then, could it possibly mean to assert that government *as such,* and as distinguished from this or that government, is or is not legitimate? Evidently it could only mean that it is, or is not, in accordance with rule. But what rule? What law? If we say, "with rules as such," or "law as such," we speak without meaning. And at that point we should be able to see, too, that there is no meaning to government as such, and hence there is nothing whose claim of legitimacy can either be confirmed or rejected. The whole problem is a philosophical fabrication comparable to asking, for example, for the dimensions of space or the duration of time.

The Problem
of Justification   XIV

Within any body politic
some men, and usually vast numbers of them, are governed by others,
usually by rather few and sometimes by only one. This is what distinguishes a body politic, such as a state, from a random assemblage. And to
say that the many are thus *governed* by the few means that these latter
have power over them, can decide certain matters of great importance
for them (even in opposition to what they would themselves have decided), can seize their property through taxation and otherwise and use it
in ways that seem to them best, can lay down rules for them to follow,
and punish them, often severely, for their failure to do so.

Government, in a word, is the coercion through threat and force of
the many by the few. This rather harsh way of putting the matter is sometimes modified by speaking of government by laws rather than by men,
or of government by the people themselves in democracies, as though
laws were not enacted and enforced by those who happen to hold power,
in democracies as well as any place else. The fact is that in no state do
men literally govern themselves. They are governed by relatively few, in
the best states as well as in the worst.

That such a relationship should exist clearly demands justification,
in case it has any. That one group of men should be able to reach into
the pockets of others through the power to tax, and spend what others
have earned in ways they might or might not approve, demands justification. That these same men should be able to present to the rest long lists
of actions that they are forbidden to do under the threat of various pains

and penalties—things which they might have wanted to do or even have felt morally obligated to do—demands justification. In short, that men should be related as sovereign and subject, that one should be compelled to bow to the will of another, usually someone wholly unknown to him, requires some sort of justification.

This is what has in political philosophy traditionally been considered to be *the* problem of government. Those of us who are not philosophers often do not feel it as a problem because we have never for a moment of our lives existed entirely free of any political order. Government has therefore conditioned our lives from the moment of our birth, and we are as accustomed to it as the air we breathe. Most persons are, moreover, more or less content with things; they find their places within the system and, for the most part, dwell there in comfort. This seems to be true even of those living under despotic rule for which any sort of philosophical justification would seem utterly hopeless, in states whose vast populations only learn by reading in a newspaper who happens at a given time to have supreme power over them. As long as men feel content with what has been thrust upon them, they have little inclination to ask why or wherefore, and sometimes when they are not content there is still little point in asking questions, for there is not much that can be done to change things.

The fabulous wanderer The following imaginative exercise will perhaps bring this basic problem to light and will also serve as a useful instrument, as we proceed, for *testing* various possible answers to this question.

Suppose you have from birth enjoyed the comfort and security of a civilized community at the southern tip of an immense island, all of the island to the north presenting an array of mountains and wilderness and, it is generally supposed, no human inhabitants. And let us imagine that you become a member of an expeditionary party organized to explore the rest of the island. After many months of endurance and struggle you reach the other end of the island and there suddenly, without any forewarning or even the slightest expectation of what was about to happen, you find yourself thrust into a society of men whose existence you had never even suspected. You soon learn, moreover, that you are expected to spend the rest of your days in this strange and forbidding place, and with that in mind your conditioning and instruction begin at once with respect not only to its strange language and cultural history but to all those things that you will and will not be permitted to do, and all the things you will have to do, from fear of dreadful consequences attending failure. You are, in fact, subjected to years and years of such training and conditioning, since the behavior patterns of this strange society are highly complex, and its rules and customs cannot be mastered easily.

Through it all, however, certain things become clear. For example, the obligations and prohibitions that are conveyed to you do not at all presuppose your assent. Some of the things you have to do are quite difficult, and a few you even consider deeply wrong, but some of the forbidden things are those you would like very much to do, or even, in the case of a few, things you would normally feel morally obligated to do. None of this matters. The rules are made up for you, and although it is hoped that you will approve of them, it is not necessary that you should. All that is necessary is that you obey them. It is also clear that these rules are made up by men you will probably never see and will know only indirectly by hearing reports of them or seeing their pictures. And finally, it is made clear that if you go along with the rules, doing as you are told and yielding up to these men what they demand, then you have a fair chance of living in comfort and security. This is by no means guaranteed, however, and in fact you may sometimes be told to risk life and limb for things important to them, though perhaps not important to you. If, on the other hand, you violate even a single one of these rules, then you will, if this is detected, risk pains and penalties, perhaps severe ones, and perhaps throughout the remainder of your life.

So much for our imaginative exercise. We shall return to it frequently as a testing ground for our theories. Meanwhile, two points must be noted.

The first is, that *if* one became a member of a society in the manner just described, he could surely ask: What is the *justification* of the arrangement under which, from no choice of my own, I now find myself? Why should I have to live like this, and by what right do these strange people compel me to?

And the second point is, that every one of us *did* become a member of the society to which we think of ourselves as "belonging"; was conditioned and taught its rules, obligations, our prohibitions; was warned with respect to its threatened pains and evils, and tempted with respect to its possible comforts and rewards, in very much the manner just described. The only significant difference is that, instead of coming from a previously existing society, and thus having to be retrained, taught, and conditioned within a brand-new one, we were thrust into this one from our mother's wombs and were therefore trained, taught, and conditioned from zero. The thoroughness and effectiveness of such conditioning reduces our need to demand a justification, but philosophically it has no relevance to this question whatever.

The avoidance of the problem   There appears to be no generally accepted answer to the problem just presented. It is possible that none exists, and that government, whatever form it might assume, simply has no justification. At least one contemporary political theorist has, on the basis of rather powerful arguments, drawn just this conclusion, as we have seen.* Yet the question does, once formulated, appear to have such overwhelming importance that one cannot help wondering why it is everywhere so lightly dismissed. Part of the answer to this, I believe, is that in the course of being conditioned to the constant and ubiquitous power of government, to the point where we no longer feel it very acutely, we are at the same time conditioned to accept the most banal justificatory formulas, slogans that are laughably false, with which we seem to be provided in order to have something or other to trot out when needed. One, for example, is that in *our* society (unlike many of those more backward) we are governed, not by men, but by laws; and further, that it is through such laws that our freedom is guaranteed rather than cancelled. Another, soberly and pompously offered for belief even by men who have grown up, is that in *our* society (unlike many of those more backward) we govern ourselves. The machinery for this may be imperfect and cumbersome, to be sure, but the laws we live under are of our own making, and their discipline is simply our own self-discipline. There is, therefore, no problem of justifying government as coercive because our government is not coercive—no man is coerced by his own will. *Other* governments are often coercive, and it is for precisely that reason that they lack justification.

The idea just expressed amounts to a purported answer to our question and will therefore be dealt with along with some other answers. Meanwhile something should be said in passing about the alleged government of the people by laws rather than by men.

It is exceedingly difficult to see how this idea could ever have gained entry into the minds of intelligent men, other than as an expression of their general contentment with things. It would be impossible, for example, to imagine such an idea springing into the mind of a southern black man in the fifties, compelled to use only the rear end of a bus, and this in the name of ordinances duly passed by a legislature or council. But the whole claim is demonstrably false by the most elementary philosophical considerations.

The philosophical impossibility of government by laws   Rules and laws do not govern, for they can compel or inhibit no one. A rule or law, whether printed, uttered, or however promulgated, is but an inanimate thing—a sound in the air or marks upon paper—and is quite incapable, by itself, of coercing any living things. At most such rules serve as guides to the coercion of men by other men. They amount to permissions to apply coercive force, but by themselves coerce neither governors nor governed.

* See Robert Wolff, *In Defense of Anarchism,* in Chapter VIII.

Thus, a traffic sign at an intersection does not compel any motorist to stop. It only serves as a symbol that some man or men—the town council, for example, or the chief of police—have made it a rule that cars stop there, and that certain unpleasant consequences are possible for those who do not. The coercive force is therefore not generated by the sign itself (this being only an inanimate and inoffensive object incapable of hurting anyone or having any will) nor by the rule in accordance with which the sign was put there (this being something likewise innocuous), but by that man or men who make the rule, cause the sign to be planted there, and in general make known their expectation of obedience.

The same is true, of course, of laws themselves. However grand in purpose and scope, and however inspiring in formulation, they have in themselves no more power to coerce to obedience, and hence no more power to govern, than the merest grain of sand. As a thing stated, or even proclaimed from the throne, a law has no force whatsoever upon anyone. Only as the expression of the will of some man or men—that is to say, of government—does it become coercive. But then it of course becomes clear that what is coercive is government, i.e., some man or men in authority, and not their laws. Common expressions such as "the Law prohibits" or "the Law requires" and so on are never literally true. They are but reminders of what someone intends to see done or avoided and of how he is capable of making things unpleasant for any who disregard that intention.

We thus have our problem, and it is not easily disposed of by slogans or platitudes. Within every legal order, whether it be a tribe of savages or a vast and powerful nation, there is a man or group of men who govern the rest, that is, who compel them to do what they would not otherwise do (for example, to hand over to them large amounts of their money, called taxes) and prevent them from doing what they would otherwise do (for instance, from helping themselves to the plenty to which their neighbor lays claim). These kinds of compulsion and constraint are always the artifice of men, and therefore they might not exist at all without any violation of nature. Oviously we may not rationally assent to such coercion without some justification for it. We might capitulate to it from fear, but this is neither assent nor justification. The vast majority of men appear to have assented without requiring any justification, or on the basis of some perfectly childish justification. We are now asking for something better.

False leads It is commonly thought that the only problem here is justifying this or that *form* of government, it being taken for granted that the institution of government itself needs no justification. But the latter is clearly the prior question; for there can be no question of justifying this or that form of government if government itself is without justification or if, as seems to be pretty much the case, the justification of it is unknown. It may indeed be that only certain governmental forms and procedures have any justification, and therefore a particular government is justified only by showing that it is of this or that kind; but this cannot be assumed at the outset. Reverting to our fabulous case of the man who stumbles into a hitherto unknown society and learns that he will be expected to spend the rest of his life there, subject to all its orders and constraints, such a man would not feel that this seemingly baneful plight had received any justification upon being assured that the legal order there is of a certain kind—a dictatorship of the proletariat, for example, or a representative democracy. He might want no part of it, even if it were proved to him to have been instituted by God.

Nor, even more obviously, is it any kind of justification to point out that a given government is *legitimate* within a society and that its commands are accordingly lawful. For in this context, "legitimate" only means lawful, and we are asking for the justification of laws themselves. Our fabulous wanderer would feel no reassurance upon learning that the ruler he is now expected to obey is the "legitimate" sovereign within that society, meaning, perhaps, that he holds title to his office through inheritance from his royal father.

Nor, finally, is it any sufficient answer to our question to trot out such familiar shibboleths as "Only under government can men be truly free," or "Law is the final protector of liberty," or "There is no real freedom except under law." There may be a truth underlying such popular watchwords, and we shall in fact see that there is, but they do not solve our problem. They cannot, for *all* government is coercive and compels those who live under it to do and to refrain, under threat of pains and forfeitures. If, then, this is the path of freedom, then we have, at the very least, a paradox to resolve. It may be that there are good and conclusive reasons why men should be governed, good reasons why they should be systematically threatened by superior force, and it *may* even be that one of the reasons for this is to enlarge and enhance their very freedom; but no philosopher can say anything so paradoxical and simply let it go at that. It does not solve the problem but only sharpens it.

Possible solutions Numberless solutions to this problem have been proposed, solutions drawn from religion, jurisprudence, economics, philosophy, and elsewhere. Of those that have attracted the greatest attention and interest in the development of political philosophy, there are four that are worth considering with some care. These are the theories of the moral justification of government, the theory of utility, the theory of self-government, and of course, the traditional theory of contract. A consideration of these will yield insight into the ethics of citizenship as well as a clearer idea of what is required for justification in this particular context.

Morality, Utility, and Self-Government XV

It is not uncommon for men to assume a kind of moral basis for a legal order, the thought being that, wherever this basis is lacking, there is likewise lacking a basic justification, and one is confronted, not with true government, but with the simple rule of force. Thus men are apt to assume that the positive legal order, the existing laws and judicial apparatus—provided they are justified—must embody, though perhaps imperfectly, certain general principles of morality and justice, expressed as respect for human life and dignity, fairness, the rights of man, the sanctity of property, and so on. The question whether this or that legal order is justified, therefore, simply turns into the question whether it does or does not uphold and promote such principles of justice and morality.

Philosophers who have been enchanted by this idea come easily to mind. Plato, of course, thought that the right of rule coincided with the degree of philosophical acumen necessary for the understanding of justice and goodness; and the thought that the unjust or wicked ruler lacks, by virtue of his very injustice, a necessary condition for the legitimacy of his rule, is an idea that is as old as the sentiment of rebellion itself. Philosophers still tend to take for granted, with Locke, that men have certain *natural* rights, which government must respect and protect, and that any society in which those rights are not protected by the legal order is one that is, *ipso facto,* ruled without justification. Such ideas as these are commonplace, and although few today would want to weave morality into the very fabric of civil government as did Plato and the German thinkers of the nineteenth century, probably even fewer would suppose that there is no essential connection at all between law and morality.

We cannot go into this view at length simply because it would involve an excursion into the whole realm of morals, a realm that is so large and dark that, once in it, it is doubtful whether we would ever emerge. The truth in′ this view overlaps with certain other claims that have been made for representative democracy or for the utilitarian basis of legislation; it would be an enormous job to sort that all out.

All we need to consider here is the pure and simple claim that the justification of a legal order, such as our own, coincides with the recognition by that order of certain natural moral principles and with the government of men in the light of those principles. And surely no such claim is tenable. The justification of a coercive legal order, in case it has any, cannot depend on any purely moral commitment of that order. If it did, then a consequence would be that no government could properly compel any citizen to do anything in violation of his own moral sentiments, no matter how strange and eccentric those might appear to others. For certainly no one actually *knows* what moral principles are true, if indeed any are true at all. The most anyone can do concerning any moral principle is express his own sentiments about it or those of some institution whose ideals he happens to share, such as the American Legion, his church, or whatever. If the legitimacy of a coercive law rests upon its coherence with a true principle of morality, then it cannot properly coerce those who find in it no such coherence. If the legitimacy of law depends upon its morality, then law must always yield to morality wherever the two conflict, or even where they merely appear to conflict—there being no way whatever of distinguishing appearance from reality in this area. Laws, accordingly, must under this philosophy be binding only upon those who approve of their content and have no coercive force upon those who do not. And this conclusion falls only slightly short of saying that there cannot be any legitimate positive laws and, hence, no justified legal order; for a law that has no application to those who choose to ignore it is no law, but at best a request or exhortation.

Perhaps the clearest way to bring out the basic difficulty in this theory of government is by our story of the fabulous wanderer. Suppose you ask by what right you are governed by men you do not even know and never see, by what right they compel you to do numberless onerous things day and night under threat of pain if you fail, and so on. And suppose you receive as an answer the following disquisition: "This commonwealth is governed by a philosopher who has worked out the true principles of justice and morality. If he says something should be done, then you can be sure that it should, even though it may appear senseless to you, for he issues his orders in the light of his understanding of morality. True, some of the things he expects of you will be burdensome. Others will seem frivolous or pointless. Some may appear to violate your own deepest moral convictions. But disregard all that. What you will be doing, if you act in accordance with his orders, will be right and just, for they are commanded by him in the light of his knowledge of what moral rightness and justice are."

The thing to note about the "justification" thus offered is that it does not serve as any justification to you, for two very good reasons. The first is that there is no way these claims could be shown to be true; and the second is that even if you could be persuaded of them, the alleged "justification" would still be lacking.

No government has any way of showing that the moral principles it honors, if any, are true. Even if it were shown that they had been upheld by the ablest philosophers, by Plato himself perhaps, or even by Kant, it would amount to no demonstration of their truth, nor even the slightest evidence to one who happens to prefer other principles. And even if one believed that this or that legal order was in fact based upon some true principle of morality or justice, that would not by itself justify its jurisdiction over him. One searches in vain for any connection between the two claims. A man's adherence to some true principle of justice does not confer on him the authority to govern anyone. It is at most a desirable quality. The declaration, "I am a wise and good man," might be followed by this other, "Therefore, I am entitled to command you, and you are obligated to obey," but the relationship of the two declarations is one of mere sequence. The word "therefore," irrelevantly appearing between them, is purely decorative and expresses no rational connection at all. To be a wise and good man is one thing. To possess the right to rule others is a different thing. The connection between the two is at best one of fond hope, not rational necessity.

The theory of utility   A closely related idea, and one that is apparently widely believed, is that government is justified by its advantage over anarchy, or what Hobbes called a "state of nature." Men living together without government cannot live in safety. They are a constant menace to each other, for without government there is no one to enforce any rules, nor in fact are there any legitimate rules to enforce. Personal safety must under such conditions depend entirely upon one's own strength, wit, and such weapons as he can lay hands on, which amounts to saying that there is no personal safety at all. Beyond this, men have many needs, over and above mere safety from day to day, which have no chance of fulfillment apart from a legal order. Commerce, communication, the construction of highways and other public devices, and all of the give-and-take between men which is to the advantage of everyone and makes civilization possible—all these things presuppose the existence of an effective legal order. Government, accordingly, is simply the price men pay for these blessings, and that is its justification—that it does secure them more or less and that they are worth what they cost, perhaps far more.

The theory is simple, plausible, and as we shall see, it expresses an important truth. But it is not sufficient as thus stated because it is over-simple.

That there is a connection between justified rule and the happiness of those ruled is clear enough. It is, in one form or another, the general appeal that is made in defense of a particular government or its policies. Similarly, any government whose policies unavoidably grind its subjects into misery lacks justification in a very clear sense. Rebellion against it would for that reason be at least defensible.

It is not enough, however, to declare that government is justified by its utility in general ways such as those adumbrated above. One must in addition specify clearly meaningful senses. Furthermore, it must then be shown that some great human good or goods can be achieved under government and not without it, for otherwise the means and the end will not be commensurate.

Thus, even though it is not false, it is not enough to say that government is justified by its usefulness. Usefulness to what end? Or that it is justified as an instrument for the achievement of human happiness, or human freedom, or the common good. These terms are altogether too vague and general. One would need to know what happiness or freedom consists of, and what is meant by the common good. Again, even when such generalities are avoided, and the specific ends attained through a governed life are set forth, these must be ends commensurate with the means to their realization. If someone offered as the justification of the modern state that it provides an efficient postal service, for example, he would speak absurdly—not because what he said would be untrue, but because means and end would be out of proportion with each other.

If we say that men are happier and better off under government than otherwise, we might be right; but why are they happier? And how better off? It is imaginable that men could be made to feel lastingly happy by ingesting some kind of drug; but exclusive possession of such a drug and the power to administer it would not justify anyone in governing by such means.

But perhaps the best way to illustrate these points is by reverting, once more, to our imagined wanderer. Suppose again he asks for some justification of the arrangement he now finds imposed upon him, and in response he is told that the society in which he finds himself is ruled, not by a wise philosopher devoted to justice and morality, but rather by one who is dedicated to human happiness, freedom, and well-being. The wanderer would perhaps greet this news with a certain sense of relief; but if he were rational, he would also perceive, first, that these grand and evocative words were so far without any specific meaning, and second, that his question had not really been answered. He did not ask: What may I expect in this place? Even if he had, the response suggested would not have been much of an answer. Instead, he asked: By what right do these people govern me? The answer he received was not totally unrelated to his question, but as thus vaguely expressed, it was largely so. Just as the claim, "I am wise and good," does not, even if true, yield the further claim, "therefore I am justified in making laws for you to obey," so likewise the claim, "My methods are effective in the production of human happiness, freedom, and well-being," similarly fails to confer authority to make laws, though not so abysmally. The response, in this case, is not something to be thrown out as irrelevant, but rather something to be enlarged and made more specific. This is what we shall shortly attempt.

The theory of self-government   Consider a man who makes out a set of rules for himself and then by his own choice abides by them, sometimes foregoing what he wants perhaps badly to do, in fidelity to his code. Now in case he really is the author of it, no problems of justifying his obedience to it arises; and that code, however severe and restraining its provisions might be, cannot be represented as tyrannizing over him to whom it is applied, or in any way coercing him in the slightest. No man can coerce himself, and this code is but the expression of his own will. The will he obeys is therefore his own and, being both sovereign and subject, he is in reality neither. He is like a man who plays checkers with himself. Such a man neither wins nor loses, precisely because he does both.

Or consider again our fabulous example. Let us suppose our wanderer, finding himself suddenly in this strange society, learns that its laws rest upon unanimous consent, that no law, therefore, can take effect in case there is a single dissent, and that any law, once enacted, becomes void the moment one citizen rejects it. No more is needed for repeal. Now in case he enters this society on these terms, and is perfectly free at any moment to take leave of it—since it would require a law to restrain him, and no such law could be effective without his consent—then there is no problem of justifying the legal order under which he then places himself. It needs no justification because it cannot coerce him, and the laws he obeys are in the fullest sense the expression of his own will. Any law that he does not regard as expressing his will ceases, by that very fact, to be law.

This, or something resembling it, is sometimes imagined to be the model of democratic society—a great town meeting where, with one mind, everything is decided by all. This was without doubt the model of liberty under government that dominated much of Rousseau's thought. The idea it perfectly embodies, that government should somehow express the will of those governed, has dominated most of the political philosophy of our tradition. Nothing short of it could really fit the formula of government of, by, and for the people. It is no wonder, then, that many have supposed democratic society to be self-justifying. In a democracy, it is thought, the people govern themselves and are accordingly free even though subject to rule. The laws by which they are governed rest upon their own consent. And just as no man can coerce himself, so no group of men can coerce themselves. Their laws might be foolish, frivolous, or even mischievous, just as the rules a man might make up for himself could be, but this in no way tarnishes their justification. No justification is needed for my "subjugation" to myself, since there is in that case no real subjugation, and the same will be true of any government that simply expresses the will of the government.

Of course the difficulty with all this is perfectly obvious—no such government has ever existed, except perhaps in the tiniest bodies politic; and if one were created to govern a nation, it would hardly last through the day. Such "government" is in fact the very denial of government, for to say that a law is nullified by the "nay" of a single subject is about the same as saying that there is no law at all. Still another way of expressing this fairly obvious point is that there is no discernible difference between a society governed in the manner just described and one not governed at all. The reason that such government requires no justification is that there exists, in this scheme, no government to justify.

Majority rule   It is from this consideration that theorists and the founders of governments have sometimes replaced the ideal of rule by *unanimity* with rule by *majority* and *plurality,* thus protecting freedom, but not at the cost of lawlessness. In this way, it is supposed, the freedom of those governed is preserved, since each has a voice in what laws shall take effect, and at the same time government is made possible. Indeed, it is very common for those living under a system of majority rule to describe themselves as *free men,* and even to suppose that the laws are made by themselves. The ideal of government *by* the people is generally thought not to be seriously compromised when this is understood to mean something less than all the people, provided, of course, those who govern constitute a majority, or at least a plurality.

If this is so—that is, if it can be maintained that the legal order and all its parts rest upon acceptance by those governed, even in case actual acceptance by more than a majority or even a plurality is not required to give that legal order its full force—then of course the justification of that order is obvious. We need only invoke again the principle that no justification is needed for a man's obedience to his own will. If the laws I am expected to obey are of my own making, I can hardly protest this expectation. And if they can still be represented as of my own making when ratified by a sufficient number, which may or may not include me, then again I can hardly protest, for their justification is implicit.

However, this line of thought is no longer available to us. It may be that democratic government conceived as majority rule has a justification, but at least its justification cannot be that, under such a form, men are placed under laws of their own making. The shift from rule by unanimity to rule by plurality or even majority does not represent merely a change of degree. It is not merely a compromise with an ideal for the sake of the practical and therefore something still possessing the same kind of justification, though it falls short of the absolute. We have, by this shift, deprived ourselves of that justification entirely.

We can imagine a man who makes up a set of rules for himself and finds that he has to compromise some of his interests in order to protect his others. He evolves a set of rules that enables him to attain most of the things he wants, but at the cost of others. Now if such a man should subsequently ask why he should continue to honor his rules when it means giving up something he wants, the answer would be clear: it is only in obedience to his own will that he makes this sacrifice in order not to lose something more precious.

But can a body politic, whose laws receive their force through ratification by a majority, be likened to this model? Not at all, and for two reasons. In the first place, from the fact that the interests overruled by the majority are the interests of a numerical minority, it by no means follows that they are minor interests. They may be the supreme interests of those overruled. And to say in such a case that the minority, deprived of what is to them supremely important out of deference to the perhaps whimsical will of the majority, is really thus deprived *in accordance with its own will*, is absurd.

And in the second place, the will that prevails under such an arrangement is by no means a *compromise* will of the entire body politic. It is instead one will totally victorious over another. It is thus highly misleading to speak of each having a voice in the enactment of law under such an arrangement. All that is promised is that the voice of each will be *heard*, however distantly. It is quite consistent with this that, once heard, it is then ignored, and its possessor compelled to do the exact opposite of what, through that voice, he was willed.

Both points can be neatly illustrated by invoking once more our fabulous wanderer. Thus we suppose him to be taken in by this strange society, and then to learn that one of its institutions, sanctioned by law democratically enacted, is the enslavement of all persons not members of the society by birth. He is to his great relief also informed, however, that this law will not apply to him without his first having a voice in the matter and unless it is found to be the expression of his own will. The question is put to the vote, everyone is given his say, including our wanderer, and it is found that a majority express preference for retaining the institution, our fabulous wanderer being, in fact, the sole dissenter. He is forthwith enslaved, deprived of every right, and at the same time solemnly told that he has not only had a *voice* in this decision, entirely on a par with every other voice that was heard, but that, in fact, the steps now taken are thus in accordance with his own will!

The absurdity of these latter claims is perfectly clear. The example is farfetched, but the point it makes is not in the least so. *Tyrannical force, whether great or small, is absolutely inherent in the principle of self-government conceived as majority rule,* for *every* law thus arrived at (except in the rare event of unanimity) will entail the forcible coercion of a minority by the majority against its will. There may be a justification for this, but if so, it has not yet been touched upon.

This difficulty of majority rule seems inherent. Nothing can remove it. But if we now take the next step toward what we actually find in the world—namely, representative government—the problem is enormously magnified. Here we find law created, not by a majority or even a plurality, but rather by a miniscule minority, whose entitlement to this role is that they were somehow "chosen" for it by a complex series of political machinations and jockeyings for power that only superficially resembles any choice by "the people." This probably introduces no new difficulties of justification, but it certainly aggravates the ones already elicited. Whatever may be the justification of this legal order, it cannot be maintained that it is the creation of those upon whom it falls, or that it is the expression of their own wills. It is purely rhetorical and poetic to call such a system one of self-government at all. It is no more such than is the government by an absolute but popular despot, and it presents exactly the same problems of justification.

The Theory of Contract   XVI

The idea that government must rest upon some original mutual consent or contract between men is as old as political theory and has always been the great favorite among philosophers. Historically the first representative of this theory seems to have been Glaucon, who appeared in Plato's *Republic* to argue that justice arose when men agreed among each other to forego the advantages of unrestrained liberty in the interests of mutual safety. Another version of the theory, based upon moral considerations, was offered by Socrates, who argued that a citizen's remaining within a given *polis* implied his acceptance of its laws. Eventually some version or other of the contract theory became the cornerstone of political philosophy, particularly in England.

It is not hard to see why it should have such an appeal. The subjection of the many to the few, which the former accept with such complacency, demands some sort of justification, in case there is any. Otherwise, government would be nothing but the expression of brute force, and obedience to law, nothing but the expression of fear. If men governed themselves there would, of course, be no problem of justification, for the will they bowed to would then be their own. Until comparatively recent times it was not possible to describe government in terms of this model without obvious absurdity, however, for men can hardly express their own will through the edicts of a king who holds sovereign power from his father, or from God, or from his army.

There is another way in which the orders one is obliged to obey can

109

be thought of as the expression of his own will, even when they are contrary to his will as he declares it—namely, where he has previously declared his willingness to abide by those orders, whatever they might turn out to be. Thus, suppose I promise to serve someone, in return, perhaps, for benefits that he shall bestow upon me. He then produces those benefits as expected and calls upon me to serve him in certain ways which I perhaps now find onerous or perhaps deeply distasteful. He of course can recall me to my promise—it is, after all, what I agreed to—and in doing so he calls upon me to perform what I have myself expressed a willingness to do. Thus what he wills is what I too have already willed, even though it may in a clear sense be contrary to my will, as I now declare it.

In that relationship there appear, many have thought, the elements of political obligation. Nothing short of some sort of prior agreement, implicit or implied, on the part of those who are governed, would seem to offer hope of justifying the rule of the many by the few. Since no man can be represented as consenting to his own enslavement, then the governance of him by others must be represented as a consequence of something else he has consented to and can therefore not now reasonably protest.

The nature of contract   The institution of contract is very old, and the practical advantages of it quite clear. Wherever civilizations have existed, men have been aware of the enormous advantages of give-and-take among themselves, of doing and being done for, whereby one often obtains great benefits to himself, sometimes at little cost. Plato thought that this was part of the very foundation of a political life. It explains better than anything else why men should come together in the first place to form any kind of association. If, however, anyone does something for someone else, and his whole reason for doing it is the expectation that he shall in turn be done for by him whom he serves, then it is absolutely essential that this expectation be a confident one, that it not rest merely on faith or trust. Thus arises the special feeling of obligation associated with a contractual relationship. One quite naturally feels exploited and taken advantage of when such expectation is disappointed, and expresses this feeling as censure and condemnation. So natural and reliable are these moral feelings and the sense of obligation that it is exceedingly rare that there exist, even in the most advanced legal systems, any positive law upholding the institution of contract, it being assumed that the obligation obtains in the absence of statute.

Now in case the relationship between sovereign and subject is one of contract, then the justification for the coercive legal order embodied in all government is quite plain. One should put up with the coercions of government simply because he has agreed to. Having received the protection and blessings of government, a citizen can have no reasonable objection to performing the sometimes onerous and even galling responsibilities of citizenship, these being simply the price, and the price he has himself agreed to pay, for the former.

The objection usually directed toward any such theory is a factual one—that is, there is no evidence that any such contract exists. Some nations can, to be sure, point to actual compacts in the earliest days of their existence; but these can hardly, even with the most permissive notions of contracts, be regarded as binding upon later generations, or as having any connection with them except as archaic curiosities. They were drawn up by a tiny handful of men ages ago and were clearly intended to express principles applicable primarily to themselves.

Perhaps this point can be made more clearly from the standpoint of the present. If it is claimed that I owe obedience to those who govern me under a contract which I have made with them, then I am certainly entitled to know its terms. But where are they found? How shall disputes concerning the respective contractual obligations of those party to it be resolved? Obviously, no such contract exists. Perhaps I do have obligations to those who govern me, perhaps they are even as extensive and detailed, and my own subjugation as profound, as seems implied by the legal order and all its oppressive machinery. But if so, this subjugation and consequent obligation cannot be represented as something *I* have consented to under contract, for no such contract exists. The whole theory rests on a fable, perhaps invented to rationalize, rather than actually justify, the fact of sovereign power.

Actually this objection has little force, for it betrays an ignorance of what a contract really is. When we think of a contract, we are apt to think of a document, possibly a long and complex one, wherein certain parties are identified, the undertakings and promises of each listed in some detail, and bearing at the end the signatures of those parties, perhaps duly witnessed. But a contract need be nothing like this, even in the most advanced and sophisticated legal system such as our own.

Verbal and implicit contracts Suppose, for example, a man telephones another and says simply: "I'm in the business of making widgets and can offer them to you this week at fourteen dollars per gross." The other, after a few questions, replies, "All right, why don't you send over a few cartons, and I'll see how they go." That's all. Now these two men have entered into a legal and formal contract in every sense of the word. Their exchange does not amount to a mere gentleman's agreement, a *quid pro quo*, or an informal swapping. It is a binding contract, even though no document was drawn up, nothing signed. The widget-maker is contractually bound to deliver and, doing so, the vendor is contractually obligated to pay him.

Or again, suppose there appears at my house one day, unsummoned, a gang of workmen and a truckload of shrubs, small trees, and similar accessories of the landscapist; and suppose that to my astonishment and delight these workmen proceed to decorate and improve my otherwise barren property, while I look on—they having evidently misinterpreted their directions and arrived at the wrong place. Their work completed, they present their bill. Do I owe them payment? Can I maintain that I did not hire them, have no contract with them, and hence no contractual obligation to pay them?

I cannot. There is no documentary contract, nor is there even a verbal agreement, nor any verbal exchange whatsoever, nor anything so informal as a handshake; but there is nevertheless a contract in the full sense. The contract is *implicit* and arises from the fact that, knowing what these men were doing and that it was a valuable service to me, I made no attempt to stop them nor to correct the error under which they were proceeding.

An implied contract of the sort just illustrated is fully enforceable in law, provided the facts are not in dispute. It is no myth of philosophers, contrived to bolster some fanciful theory of government. It is a legally binding arrangement even though there are neither written nor spoken words of a contractual nature.

For what, essentially, *is* a contract? It is a mutual promising in exchange for mutual service. It is not a document, nor any utterance. The latter is only the expression of the contract, and the importance attached to a written document is only a consequence of the importance of knowing, after the fact, what it is that was promised, so that a third person, such as a judge, not party to the contract, can know its terms. It seems to be in this fashion that the common notion arose that agreements in writing are *more binding* than others, the obligation to uphold them therefore more strict, and the breach of them more blameworthy. This is not so. It is not that these are more binding, but simply that they are more easily enforced.

Social contract   Can we, then, find here the basis for justifying the coercive power of the state over its citizens? True, I never explicitly agreed to obey the restrictions of those who make laws for me, never explicitly agreed to deliver up to the state part of my goods, possibly even my own safety, in return for the supposed blessings it bestows upon me; but have I not, perhaps, *implicitly* agreed to all that?

This claim was eloquently and with perfect clarity expressed by Socrates. It still has its defenders, but no one has ever succeeded in expressing it better than Socrates.

Approached by his friend Crito in his prison, where he was awaiting the execution of the death penalty that had been judicially imposed on him, Socrates was exhorted to flee, to place himself out of the reach of his persecutors, and not submit to, and pay for with his life, the injustices of those who governed Athens. He had, his friend claimed, no obligation to cooperate with injustice and to pay so high a price to those forces of wickedness to whom he assuredly owed nothing. Escape, moreover, would be easy and would undoubtedly be welcomed by the very authorities who had condemned him to death.

Socrates' answer to these solicitations amounts to an eloquent and even inspiring defense of the theory of an implicit contract. He personifies the laws, and then represents them as addressing him as follows:

Then consider, Socrates [he has the laws say] if we were right in saying that by attempting to escape you are attempting an injustice. We brought you into the world, we raised you, we educated you, we gave you and every other citizen a share of all the good things we could. Yet we proclaim that if any man of the Athenians is dissatisfied with us, he may take his goods and go away wherever he pleases; we give that privilege to every man who chooses to avail himself of it, so soon as he has reached manhood, and sees us, the laws, and the administration of our state. No one of us stands in his way or forbids him to take his goods and go wherever he likes, whether it be to an Athenian colony or to any foreign country, if he is dissatisfied with us and with the state. But we say that every man of you who remains here, seeing how we administer justice, and how we govern the state in other matters, has agreed, by the very fact of remaining here, to do whatsoever we tell him. And, we say, he who disobeys us acts unjustly on three counts: he disobeys us who are his parents, and he disobeys us who reared him, and he disobeys us after he has agreed to obey us, without persuading us that we are wrong. Yet we did not tell him sternly to do whatever we told him. We offered him an alternative; we gave him his choice either to obey us or to convince us that we were wrong. . . . Are we [then] right, or are we wrong, in saying that you have agreed not in mere words, but in your actions, to live under our government? . . . [And] are you not breaking your contracts and agreements with us? And you were not led to make them by force or by fraud. You did not have to make up your mind in a hurry. You had seventy years in which you might have gone away if you had been dissatisfied with us, or if the agreement had seemed to you unjust.

But you preferred neither Sparta nor Crete, though you are fond of saying that they are well governed, nor any other state, either of the Greeks or the Barbarians. You went away from Athens less than the lame and the blind and the crippled. Clearly you, far more than other Athenians, were satisfied with the state, and also with us who are its laws; for who would be satisfied with a state which had no laws? And now will you not abide by your agreement? If you take our advice, you will, Socrates; then you will not make yourself ridiculous by going away from Athens.*

This disquisition of Socrates' is not only eloquent but persuasive. If my every action implies acceptance of a certain arrangement, and I readily partake of the benefits to myself of that arrangement, then it would be superfluous for me to declare my consent in words. The bargain I have made is implicit. Exactly the same thought is often applied to dissenters today, who are exhorted to uphold the prevailing values of our society, even on those occasions when they personally would reject them, or take leave of the society—"Love it," signs say, "or leave it."

We thus arrive at a plausible answer to our question. Why should I put up with a legal order which I did not create, whose laws and policies are the creation of persons over whom I have no real control and only the most tenuous influence? Because I have agreed to, in return for my own fulfilled expectations. It is only my part of the bargain, and that I have struck such a bargain is clear from the fact that I have remained within this jurisdiction and enjoyed the blessings of its legal order, well knowing what my own responsibilities were, when I could at any time have betaken myself elsewhere, in case I did not like the arrangement. Having made this bargain, I may not now try to back out of it when my own turn to perform has come.

The defects of this theory   I think we can best see the shortcoming of this theory by returning for a moment to our earlier fable. Consider two quite different ways in which our wanderer might become a lifelong member of that strange society into which he has stumbled.

In the first place, we can suppose that he is a fugitive or defector from his original homeland, and that coming unexpectedly upon this foreign culture, he seeks sanctuary there. Suppose this is granted, that he is promised security, in return for which it is explained to him that he

---

* From Plato: *Euthyphro, Apology, Crito*, trans. by F. J. Church, revised by Robert D. Cumming, copyright © 1948, 1956, by The Liberal Arts Press, Inc., reprinted by permission of The Bobbs-Merrill Co., Inc.

will be expected to obey all its laws, pay taxes, and perform whatever other duties are lawfully imposed on him. And finally, let us suppose he agrees. Now it is proper to say that his subjection to the rule of that government has been justified. He has agreed to it. The relationship is contractual, in every sense of the term.

Or again, we can suppose that our wanderer, though in no way restrained or prevented from leaving, does remain in this society, saying that he fears persecution if he returns to his homeland, and in any case would rather live here than any place else. No sanctuary is explicitly offered to him, but it is given, and no move to extradite him is commenced. The wanderer, largely out of gratitude for the safety he has found there, complies with the laws of the state and pays his taxes.

Here again, it is proper to say his subjection to the rule of that government has been justified. He has in every significant sense agreed to it simply by accepting, through his actions, both its advantages and its responsibilities when he did not have to. The relationship is again contractual, though the contract is an implied one.

Third, let us suppose that our wanderer, having stumbled into this place, finds that he is simply expected to do whatever he is told by those in authority, however contrary to his own desires and judgment these things might be. He is not asked whether he chooses to remain and accept subjugation by them, and he finds that they have made it overwhelmingly difficult to leave, perhaps to the point of practical impossibility.

Here the resemblance to a contractual arrangement begins to fade, and at the same time, the resemblance of the wanderer's situation to our own becomes more apparent. We begin to see, too, the extent to which the situation of the wanderer and our own resembles that of a prisoner. To complete this image of imprisonment—which cannot by the most far-fetched imagination be represented as resting on contractual arrangement —let us suppose that our wanderer was simply delivered into this place, without asking to be taken there nor even being consulted about it, and that it is an island whose surrounding waters are of near-freezing cold the year round and everywhere torn by violent currents. And now let us suppose that the wanderer is solemnly told that the coercions he suffers are a consequence of his own agreement, that he has entered into a contract involving his acceptance of this state, that it is an implicit contract whose validity rests upon the fact that he is, after all, at any time free to leave in case he rejects its conditions. The absurdity of such a declaration is too obvious to dwell on.

Is our own situation, then, like that of a party to a contract, who freely agrees to render to the other party certain things of value, out of consideration of the advantages to himself of doing so? Or does it more resemble that of a prisoner who has no choice whatever but to obey?

Surely it is the latter, and the fact that we do not normally *feel* like prisoners shows only that we have learned to put up with things. This last fanciful description could in fact serve as a fairly accurate description, entirely correct as far as it goes, of the manner in which each of us did in fact come under the coercive force of a legal order. We were quite literally delivered into it, and from then on expected to absorb its values, yield to its discipline, honor it, and comply with all its laws, under threat supported by titanic force, and without the slightest pretense that any agreement to do so was ever obtained or sought, the very idea of this being entirely fabulous. The fanciful character of such a notion is not greatly reduced by introducing the idea of an *implied* contract that is claimed to have been ratified by the sheer fact of one's continued physical presence within the domain into which he was born. For the fact, as contrasted with the abstract legalism, is that almost every man normally has countless reasons for remaining within his homeland, reasons often having nothing whatever to do with his acceptance of its legal order, and reasons of such enormous importance to him that they are likely to prevail in all but the most calamitous circumstances.

The involuntary character of large bodies politic   There are political associations that are implicitly contractual, such as those of voluntary membership in small bodies politic. If, for example, a man joins a club, chosen from a variety of others, any of which he might have joined, and then remains in it, knowing its principles, purposes, and regulations, then it can be said quite properly that he implicitly concurs with those principles, purposes, and regulations, though he may never avow them, and though his understanding of some of them may be vague. He did not have to join that club; he did not have to join any club; having joined, he did not have to remain in it. In such a context, the theory of an implied consent, even an implied contract, is perfectly plausible, even unavoidable.

The same line of thought cannot be applied to most other societal memberships, however, because there are reasons, sometimes overwhelmingly important ones, for such membership other than simple endorsement of a group's principles and rules. One cannot say, for example, that a man's mere membership in a business firm implies endorsement of that firm's policies, and hence a contractual agreement to pursue them; his membership may be an economic necessity and may have only a superficial resemblance to something contractually entered into and maintained. If a man has the choice between signing a contract or surrendering up something of supreme importance to himself, perhaps even perishing, then there is of course a clear sense in which he has entered into a contract— but we should not overlook the fact that this is in truth hardly more than a ritual performance.

When we consider membership in a *nation*—a nation into which one has in all likelihood been *born*—the resemblance to contractual association, even implicit, vanishes altogether. There are usually countless reasons for retaining allegiance to one's homeland, sometimes even in the face of enormous discouragements and disillusionments, and many of these reasons inevitably are prior in importance to any presumed endorsement of its political institutions. All of one's childhood associations are there. His kinsmen are there, and numberless things that are dear to him, which have nothing whatever to do with the legal order. He shares its customs and has imbibed its culture, he knows its language and in all likelihood knows no other. The reasons for one's attachement to his homeland could go on indefinitely without mentioning any approval of its legal order. Even if there is such approval, it is almost certainly something far down on the list, superseded by many things that have no relation at all to government.

It is, then, a completely distorting oversimplification to suppose that *the* reason for a man's membership in a nation must be his endorsement of its legal order, and that his approval and acceptance of it must be quite voluntary on the ground that, if this were not the case, he could simply leave. It is more likely that, for practical reasons, he cannot leave; and even if he could, he would not, in spite of the fact that he may abominate its legal order. His relationship to the legal order under which he lives, and the justification of its power over him, can no more be contractual than can the relationship of a child to his parents. If one imagines a tyrannical father telling his ten-year-old that, in case he does not like the cruel and oppressive regime of the home, he is free to leave, and then interpreting the child's implied rejection of that "option" as his endorsement of the first alternative, the absurdity would be quite obvious. Interpreting a man's mere continued physical presence within his homeland as implicit contractual acceptance of its legal order is hardly less absurd.

Government as an Activity XVII

The ultimate justification of the state, if it has any, can only be its expansion and enhancement of freedom. This is the unqualified good, and the necessary condition for the realization of any goodness, as we have already seen. The pursuit of any other end, subordinating the greater to some lesser good, at the expense of human freedom, is the perversion of government. A man can be deprived of the sovereignty that he has over himself by nature—of the unencumbered obedience to his own will—only by violence, never by reason, concord, or justice. One who voluntarily submits to the authority of the state can rationally do so only in the recognition that his freedom or sovereignty is not thereby cancelled or compromised, but strengthened. He can never rationally say: I hereby surrender that freedom as the price to be paid for something more precious. There *is* nothing more precious.

Viewed this way, it is no wonder that the basic problem of government, the justification of rule, has seemed so difficult, and that some have even despaired of solving it at all. The state does not at all resemble, at least on first examination, any instrument for the enhancement of freedom. On the contrary, coercion is inseparable from it, and this is plainly antithetical to freedom. The appropriate image of the state is that of a hierarchy of authority that reaches to a supreme authority or sovereign power and is enforced at every level by the overwhelming force of a leviathan. To say, then, that through *this* means the freedom of the citizen is expanded would appear, on the face of it, enormously paradoxical. It would seem that if the state can only be justified as a means for the enlargement of individual freedom, then it cannot be justified at all.

Yet we shall see in these concluding remarks that this *is* its justification, and that, notwithstanding appearances, the state, even with all its seemingly oppressive apparatus and numberless laws that are enforced at every turn by threats, can in fact be the guarantor of individual freedom. To think of men, sovereign over themselves by nature, relinquishing that sovereignty to a state and thus yielding up their freedom in exchange for something else that the state promises, is to turn reality upside down. It is within the state, and by means of it alone, that individual freedom is not merely secured but, to a large extent, found. The state does not divest its subjects of their freedom; it does not even, merely, protect their freedom. To a considerable extent, it makes such freedom possible to begin with. It is our concluding task, then, to see how this can be possible, despite so many contrary appearances.

If the state can guarantee individual freedom, it cannot be just *any* state. Probably no state in the history of the world has actually measured up to this, and very likely most governments, instead of enhancing the freedom men naturally possess, have actually done violence to it—many to the point of making slaves of their subjects. However, it is possible for the state to serve this end, and in fact, a large degree of individual freedom is not possible otherwise. Our task, then, is to show how a state renders this freedom possible, and how, accordingly, it has a rational justification.

The two aspects of freedom   Human freedom has both a positive and a negative aspect, according to what one is *permitted* to do, and what one is *enabled* to do. Most who have considered the matter have supposed that freedom is measurable in terms of the first, or permissive, aspect alone— or in other words, that one is free to the extent that there are no restraints or obstacles to his activities. But this is clearly not so. A man might remain quite unfree even in the absence of all such obstacles or restraints, for he might lack the means to do what he wants to do. Thus even in a state of anarchy men might still be slaves—not slaves of the state, to be sure, since there would be no state to enslave them, but slaves to those constant tasks necessary to the mere feat of staying alive from day to day, burdens which civil government might, to a large extent, easily lift. This double aspect of freedom can be quite easily illustrated, as follows.

Suppose, for example, one wants to travel a considerable distance, and that his doing so is in no way forbidden or prevented. Is he then free to do it? Not necessarily, for he may lack the means of accomplishing this—there may be no road to the place where he wants to go, no public transportation, and no other way of getting there.

Again, suppose one wishes to make a bequest and is not in any way forbidden to do so. Is he then free to do it? Not at all, for there may be no means; for example, the law may contain no provisions for bequests, wills, and so on, in which case nothing one does can count as making a bequest. One is thus unfree to do something, not because of the law, but precisely because there is no law.

Or once more, suppose someone, being childless, wishes to adopt children, and that the law places no obstacles in the way. This lack of laws does not enable him to do it, for by its very silence it provides no means. One might suppose that, in the absence of law, he could just go ahead and adopt children as he pleased without having to deal with red tape and bureaucrats, but of course this is not so. Nothing he might do would count as adopting a child. He might, to be sure, go around gathering up homeless children and bringing them home; but then someone else might gather up the same children a week later, and he would have accomplished nothing at all.

Or finally, suppose a man wishes to keep hunters from his farm, having decided to make it a refuge for wildlife. There may be nothing in the law or elsewhere that prohibits him from doing this as he pleases, but this does not mean that he is free to do it. He cannot, for example, even give meaning to the idea of *his* farm or distinguish it from anything else in the countryside, without a title or deed which defines its boundaries and law which protects his claims to it. Without these, every hunter in the county is perfectly entitled to demolish the woodlands as he pleases and slaughter away to his heart's content, having at least as much right to these lands as their "owner"; for without law, and the state to enforce it, no meaning can be given to the idea of an owner.

We thus see that not all law is of the form of prohibition. It has also the form of enablement, and there are countless things one is helpless to do in its absence. Freedom can hardly consist of helplessness, or ever be in the least improved by it. Freedom, in its positive aspect, is therefore impossible except under law, from which it of course follows that it is impossible except within the framework of a legal order. The idea of anarchism is therefore absurd, and it is significant that those who have spoken warmly of this idea, with much singing and genuflection to the ideal of human freedom, have generally thought of the law as consisting solely of the criminal law. They have simply taken for granted the civil law and the endless things men are enabled to do by its means, naively imagining that these things would still be right there, unaffected, even in its absence. In truth, one could not so much as mail a postcard or buy a newspaper were it not for the vast and complex mechanisms made possible only within a legal order.

What remains, then, is to sketch the broad features of a rationally justified state, its justification being its effectiveness as an instrument of freedom. That a legal order is necessary for the attainment of such freedom is clear from what has just been said, but what that legal order should be, and whether there might be alternative forms having different justifications, have yet to be considered.

Government considered as an activity   Modern democratic government should be thought of, not so much as a sovereign power that delivers edicts and laws to the masses of its citizens usurping their right to make their own decisions and annulling their freedoms, but rather as an activity carried on at various levels. Like any activity it has certain ends or purposes, sometimes good and sometimes bad, which it achieves sometimes effectively and well, sometimes ineptly and ill. In the light of these it can itself be judged as good or bad, and its justification thus found, or found wanting.

Many of the philosophical problems of government arise from a distorted conception of it, a conception gleaned largely from reading the classical political philosophers. These writers thought of government as a relationship of ruler to ruled, sovereign to subject, master to servant—a conception that was once essentially correct, even in the cases of those nations that have since evolved into modern democracies. All government was once, and in many contemporary cultures still is, the subjugation of the many to the few. In obeying the law men were, to a large extent, simply heeding the will of their sovereign. Taxes were owed to the sovereign, the tax collector was his hireling, and if any revenues were used to purchase benefits for the people this was a beneficence. Of course no one would pretend that even democratic social and political life has changed so drastically that this conception of government has become totally false, but it is, nevertheless, a distortion. If governed life were simply life subjugated to overpowering rule, then the philosophical problems of justification would be insuperable, and anarchism would be the only political doctrine rationally defensible.

The conception of government, or "the state," as a master and great father of all and a deliverer of rules or commands, and of the governed, or "the people," as its children and servants, is thus archaic at best. A servant, for example, places himself under a master, and the relationship is justified by a tacit or explicit contract voluntarily entered into. If government is conceived after this model, then the philosopher naturally looks for a contract here, too, to justify it. Of course he does not find it, for there is no social contract. This has not prevented philosophers from imagining one and even asserting that it exists as a thing of reason if not of fact, thereby generating much charming but fabulous philosophy. Here, as so often, necessity has been the mother of invention.

Similarly, a parent has a natural dominion over his children to a certain age, and the justification of this is so apparent that it is seldom stated. Parents, generally, act in the interests of their children, even at the expense of their own interests. They thus express "the will" of their children, even though the latter may not know what this is. To look at modern democratic government according to this paternalistic model is again to generate philosophical problems, simply because of the distortion in their presuppositions.

Theocratic societies, to be sure, which are governed according to the precepts discovered in certain sacred writings, do presuppose the propriety of paternalistic rule. Those governed may not always know what is their own good, but the sacred texts serve as a guide to this. It was thus once possible to put a man to death "for his own good," heeding the precepts of those texts.

Contemporary theocracies   When one thinks of government in such terms today, he is likely to think of retarded Islamic cultures, remote Tibet, or of small theocratic cultures within the larger secular state such as the Amish and Mennonite peoples, but in fact certain contemporary socialist states present clearer examples. Like every theocratic state they rest their authority on certain sacred writings that are believed to serve as reliable guides to what is good for the masses, whether this is understood by the latter or not. Indeed, these sacred writings are claimed even to express the will of the people, though this may not be known to them. Such states have their priesthood and, usually, their supreme oracle, living or dead, whose recorded thoughts are treated as devotional literature. They have their saints whose relics are sometimes preserved so that future generations may taste the holiness derived from viewing them; and for decades countless thousands pass solemnly in line to do this, imbibing their magic. They have their orthodoxies, schisms, and their heretics—now called revisionists —these being, as always, anyone whose interpretation of scripture departs from their own. Millions, through their government, profess willingness to die for the true faith, as this has been given to their forefathers, or, preferably, to keep bright the opportunity for other millions to do so. The fact that these contemporary theocracies profess scorn and hostility to religion should not at all obscure their own theocratic character, for it is only a hostility to competing faiths, not to faith itself, this being their own foundation. Persons nurtured in democratic and open cultures look upon this spectacle with incomprehension, sometimes with pity and bemusement, sometimes with horror. Occasionally serious scholars study the sacred writings upon which it rests, thinking to discover the rationale of it. To some extent they miss the point. The justification of the contemporary socialist dictatorship is precisely that of every theocracy: That those who govern do so in the interest of the governed, as this is revealed in scripture. All that is required is the faith to receive this teaching. With that, every problem of justification evaporates.

The quest for justificatory formulas If the gods have commissioned certain men to rule, or if those who rule are descended from the gods (and therefore granted some special right to rule), then those men may indeed be entitled to rule, given certain familiar presuppositions concerning the nature of the gods. They rule by a kind of right and not by mere force. Unfortunately, we have no way of knowing that the gods have thus commissioned anyone, nor for that matter, whether there are any gods in the first place, so justification along this line offers little hope. Nor, in fact, is it very often claimed anymore, though vestiges of it have lingered in recent history, even in so modern an industrial nation as Japan.

In the face of such theological doubts, it may be claimed that some wise philosophers and prophets have conferred upon certain men or classes of men the right to govern, having in mind particular ends that have been vouchsafed to the faithful, such as the final triumph of the working class. And of course this justification, unlike the theological one, is often claimed, even by great and powerful nations, as just noted. Unfortunately, although the existence of such prophets is beyond dispute, their wisdom is not, so there is no way of knowing that the texts and teachings upon which such rule is based are true. Like the theological justification, then, this one rests upon faith or, as some would prefer, upon ideology. Indeed it is hardly an accident that those governments whose claims to authority are thus defended have without exception been originally erected upon ignorance, illiteracy, poverty, injustice, and terror.

Or again, in the case of any nation whose subjects have themselves voluntarily submitted to rule, promising to obey in return for benefits promised by their rulers, we need not search far for a justification. It is based upon contract, and its parties have no grounds for complaint, provided each side keeps his part of the bargain. But government according to this pattern is more easily found in books than in the world, so there is little hope in that direction.

And finally, in case there is any nation whose rulers can make no decision and promulgate no command or law without first ascertaining, by referendum or otherwise, that they are thereby expressing the actual will of those governed, then such government requires no special justification. The people in such a nation literally govern themselves, their "rulers" being no more than their puppets, the instruments by which their own will is carried into effect. Unfortunately, however, no such nation exists; and although democratic states often profess to be so governed, they are not, as we have seen.

Justification in terms of ends   What, then, *is* the justification of government? Must we rest content with myths concerning government by the people, or the classless society, or whatnot? Is it possible that government, of whatever kind, is without real justification, that we merely spin out myths and slogans to give this or that type of rule some semblance of justification?

We shall consider a type of justification of a kind of legal order somewhat different from what is usually attempted, by emphasizing the various ends or purposes of government rather than formal structures or methods of generating law. What counts, it is suggested, is not how government arises to begin with, how men come to be chosen to govern, how laws come to be made, and so on, but rather what government accomplishes that men cannot accomplish without it.

Freedom and the Criminal Law XVIII

Let us begin, then, by taking seriously the suggestion that man is by nature a social or "political" animal. Like the tenants of an anthill, a social life is as natural to men as their erect stature, their ability to fabricate tools, and their capacity to laugh. Such things as these are not chosen, and neither is government. It is a partial misrepresentation to think of government as a purely human creation. Its various forms and structures are of human creation, but they are all variations upon something that is not, namely, social life itself, which is of necessity life within a legal order of one kind or another. Human deference to rule, which is everywhere one of the most conspicuous of human traits, is no corruption of human nature, but part of the expression of that nature.

This observation solves no real problems of justification, but it at least gets us over the first step. In the light of it we can see that the problem is not that of justifying government as such, but rather, this or that form of it. We are by nature social, but this does not mean that any social arrangement is as good as another. It only means that no philosopher needs to feel called upon for a defense of government in opposition to its absence.

Let us next, then, assume a governmental arrangement having a certain form rather like some of those that are found in the world, and then see what does in fact justify that arrangement.

We suppose, then, a legal order having the following two basic features: *First,* its public officials are responsible, in this double sense:

That while they need not in any literal sense be *chosen* by the citizens, in whose name they act, nevertheless (a) what they do in an official capacity is open and subject to public scrutiny and unrestricted criticism, and (b) their tenure of office may be terminated by those governed, either directly or indirectly, by procedures not overwhelmingly difficult to invoke—for example, through popular election or the vote of a parliamentary majority. And *second,* its criminal law is generated according to the principle of liberty described earlier—that is, nothing is made criminal by law that is not a fraud, theft, or assault, nothing that is not naturally injurious to others.

This second feature ensures that the state we are describing does not compromise the freedom of its citizens, but on the contrary enlarges it. This by itself destroys the chief philosophical criticism often leveled against it. The freedom of citizens is protected, not by any formal arrangements for the selection of rulers (such as popular election or whatnot), nor by any formal arrangement for the generation of the criminal law (such as majority or unanimous consent, enactment by chosen representatives), nor in fact by any formal features whatsover. It is, rather, protected by adherence to the principle of liberty. In substance there is, in this state, only *one* criminal law, which reads: Do not injure. The first expansion of that law is this threefold one: Do not steal, assault, or defraud. As expanded further into particular criminal laws that prohibit particular actions and threaten punishment, it remains simply an application of the basic prohibition of injury. The only freedom that is curtailed is, therefore, the freedom to injure.

The first feature—the responsibility of public officials—simply ensures that the various ends and purposes sought by the state shall be more or less generally known, at least to the extent that they are not kept secret, and that these will be more or less in keeping with the ends and purposes of the people themselves. Perfection here is not needed, nor is it necessary to be fastidious with respect to its mechanism. Not everyone needs to know from one day to the next, for example, who is doing what; it is only necessary that this be generally and approximately known, and that knowledge not be withheld from anyone who may inquire. What is important here is not the formal mechanism for the choice of public officials, but rather the ease with which they can be called to account. It is not important that men in any literal sense govern themselves, or even that they approximate it through an elaborate and carefully guarded system of representation. It is not even essential that they know from moment to moment who their lawmakers are, or be in any sort of communication with them at all. What is important is that these lawmakers, at whatever level, can be called upon to explain and justify what they have done, on pain of losing their office, that they not be protected from the criticism of those for whom they profess to act. Their wisdom is not enough, even if it is conceded to be vast. Their goodness is not enough, even if beyond question. Their honesty is not enough, even when beyond doubt. These qualities mean very little in a ruler or lawmaker who can lapse from them without fear of criticism or loss of position.

The protection of freedom through the criminal law   With respect first, then, to the criminal law—the law that defines crimes and offenses and provides punishment for the commission of them—has a state which imposes such law on its citizens a justification? It has, provided that law is generated in the manner just described, and its justification is precisely the protection of freedom which it is sometimes accused of abrogating. A man who wishes, for one reason or another, to injure his neighbor and is prevented from doing so by the state and its criminal law is deprived of a certain freedom, to be sure; but it is almost too obvious to mention that under criminal law the freedom of his neighbor is thereby greatly enlarged, and taking the two together, there is an enormous net gain of freedom. We occasionally see what happens to human freedom when the enforcement of the criminal law breaks down so that there is no effective law, or the citizens have doubt of its effectiveness. When, for example, a family is found murdered, and the assailants are known to be still at large, citizens in areas for miles around are caught up in terror and the feeling of helplessness; they are afraid to venture out without laborious precautions, to go to bed without leaving their homes and yards brightly illuminated, or to go about any of the ordinary business of life without gnawing dread and distrust. This is no picture of freedom, but a picture of the opposite— not bondage to any state, but to those forces, real and imagined, that are let loose the moment the criminal law of the state is withdrawn or weakened, or even widely believed to be such. If under these circumstances there should suddenly appear swarms of police officers, heavily armed and stationed every quarter of a mile or so, this would not be viewed by anyone as an overwhelming threat to freedom, but on the contrary, the securing of it. They might now again go about their affairs with some assurance and sense of safety, where before they could not.

The point is that the criminal law nourishes freedom rather than compromising it, provided it is enacted and enforced according to the principle of preventing injury. Though it may be vast in its scope and resolutely enforced by armed servants of the state, this does not detract from it as an instrument of freedom. These are superficial features of that law as far as freedom is concerned. What does matter is that it should reflect precisely the principle of liberty. It is in that case not, as it is sometimes represented as being, a *compromise* of freedom for the sake of security, but the enlargement and enhancement of freedom itself, and even something absolutely essential to it. The only freedom that is thus threatened is the freedom to injure; but the freedom of him who would suffer injury in the absence of law is not merely protected; it is even, to some extent, the creation of such criminal law. An appropriate image of freedom is not that of men dwelling in nature unencumbered by the familiar apparatus of government, but rather, these men in the very midst of that apparatus, and even with armed and uniformed police officers ubiquitously present. It is a strange image, but it makes this important point: That it is not the criminal law and its efficient and vigorous enforcement that enslaves, but the absence of such law, or its creation and enforcement in the light of ill-conceived principles.

The criminal law and democratic procedures   Finally, with respect to this freedom from injury protected by the criminal law, it must be noted that it has nothing whatever to do with democracy or any other governmental form. The second feature of the state we are envisioning—that its criminal law is generated according to the principle of liberty—could as well be possessed by a hereditary despotism as by a representative democracy, though in fact it is far more likely to be a feature of the latter. Thus there could, in principle, be a society governed by a despot whose political power was absolute, and whose title to govern was, for example, hereditary —a society as remote, in other words, from democratic forms and procedures as one might wish—but one whose citizens enjoyed more personal and social freedom than in any democracy that has ever existed. This would be true if that despot enunciated criminal law in faithful adherence to the principle of liberty that has been described. There is no reason why he could not do so just as effectively as the most enlightened and well-ordered democracy. History certainly suggests that this is not what one should expect from a despotic form of government, but there is nevertheless no reason, in principle, why it might not exist, why such a despot might not, in other words, consider the freedom of his subjects to be the aim of the criminal law, and promulgate such law accordingly. The important implication of this is that the justification of government, in terms of human freedom, is to be sought not in its form, but in its ends or purposes. The two tend in fact to be connected, such that a state having the first of the two features we set forth (democratic procedures) tends also to have the second (good criminal law), but they need not be. Either feature can exist without the other, and to that extent a despotic government *can* sometimes have a justification in terms of its ends, and a democratic one lack that same justification. Democratic forms and procedures are not, as they are widely thought to be, precious in themselves and hence an appropriate goal for every nation. On the contrary, when established on a foundation of ignorance and illiteracy they can be deeply pernicious.

Such democratic forms are to be desired only where they offer promise, as they sometimes but not always do, of fostering liberty through, among other things, the generation of criminal law according to the principle of liberty. Otherwise they are mere forms, subject to every abuse, and no blessing to their people at all. It is the ends or purposes of a legal order that are important, not its form. Hence the criticism of any government that it is undemocratic in form is by itself of little weight or significance.

Civil Law as a Creator of Freedom XIX

What, then, of the other aspect of freedom, the freedom of *enablement?* Is this fulfilled merely through the generation of criminal law in accordance with the principle of liberty?

It is to some extent, but to a very limited extent. As long as the principle of liberty is observed by the author of law, whoever this may be, then two results follow. The first is that those subject to the law are not prevented by law and are, to that extent, enabled to do whatever they please, short of inflicting natural injury. And the second is that they are similarly not prevented by the threat of natural injury from their fellows and are, to that extent, likewise enabled to do whatever they please, short of inflicting natural injury.

To illustrate, suppose a man wishes to undermine religion by speaking out against it, persuading his fellows, rightly or not, that the church is corrupt and its faith a pretense. He cannot be enjoined from doing this if the criminal law applicable to him is in keeping with the principle of liberty, for such speech inflicts no natural injury on anyone, however much it may damage the sensibilities. To that extent he is enabled to speak out—the law imposes no obstacles. This would be of little value to him, however, if the law did not *also* restrain his hearers who might otherwise set upon him and silence him. The same criminal law, therefore, must protect him from this and, again to that extent, enable him to speak out.

But clearly this is not enough. Freedom of enablement is not sufficiently served merely by the removal of obstacles to its exercise. There is also required the provision of *means,* for many of men's ends, particularly in view of the advanced state of modern technology, are unattainable just on the strength of the resources they happen to find at hand. One can, to be sure, speak, requiring only the means provided by nature; and one can move about, rise and sit, till his fields, come and go, and so forth without help from the law, other than simple protection. But he cannot always peacefully settle a dispute with his neighbor, keep trespassers from demolishing his fields, nor even do anything so simple as post a letter without the positive help of the state, which alone can effectively provide the means to these ends.

It is surprising the extent to which this has been overlooked by political theorists, who tend to think of the laws primarily as criminal laws—that is, as prohibitions that emanate from some sovereign authority and express the will of that authority, and only indirectly, if at all, the will of those to whom such commands are given. Thinking in these terms it is no wonder some want to endorse Jefferson's apothegm that a government is best which governs least, or Thoreau's that a government is best which governs not at all. Even J. S. Mill, in his great essay, conceived liberty to consist almost entirely in the absence of restraint by government or society.

What, then, are men enabled to do by living in a legal order or state that they would otherwise be unable to do, over and above merely dwelling in relative safety from injury? This question invites the enumeration of the proper goals of the state other than the basic one of protecting its citizens, and such an enumeration, to be complete, would have to be exceedingly and tiresomely long. What we shall do, then, is list a few of the more significant of these ends, sufficient to make our point that the freedom of enablement is to an enormous extent the creation of the state and a final reason for its existence. There is no significance in the order in which these ends or functions are listed, and no attempt will be made to assess their relative importance.

Three examples 1. The state provides for the settlement of disputes by means more decorous than the use of clubs. Thus, if my neighbor has carelessly or perhaps wantonly injured or killed my cattle and thereby exposed me and my family to the danger of hunger and want, I can do any of three things: (a) I can guard my resentment, restrain my impulse to retribution, and salvage what I can to try to survive with my family; or (b) I can assault my neighbor, take from him more or less the equivalent of what he has taken from me, and perhaps burn his house too for good measure; or (c) I can sue him for the recovery of the damage he has done me. There is not much else I can do, other than pray to the gods for help.

It is clear enough which course holds the greater promise, and no less clear that such a course of action would not even exist if the means were not provided by the civil law of the state.

2. The state, and only the state, can regulate certain resources and facilities in which all, or nearly all, have a common interest, and which would otherwise be threatened. Examples of this come readily to mind. For example, many species of wildlife would be quickly eradicated were it not for the protection of the state. Men in general agree that such wildlife should be preserved, that hunting, fishing, and other incursions into the environment should be closely regulated for the good of all, and yet only the state, through the creation and enforcement of law, can provide such protection and regulation. Often animal species are sought the more diligently by hunters just because they are rare, a high premium being placed on their feathers or furs for this reason. Without the intervention of the state there would be an unrestrained competition for these, followed soon by total extinction. Men do not voluntarily restrain themselves from such temptation; and even if hunters agreed to a man that a given species of animal should never be hunted, they would nevertheless hunt it simply from the justified conviction that if they did not, others would. A good will, even though it may be almost universal, and the endorsement of a common aim, however firmly agreed to, are not sufficient in cases like these; for the best of wills rapidly collapses in the presence of a threat to the common aim, and as if by a chain reaction, order disintegrates into a mad scramble for spoils. The state, and only the state, can enable men to achieve what all or most of them want in such cases.

3. A similar example is the pollution and corruption of the environment, which makes it not only unhealthful to all but rats, roaches, and scavengers, but noisy, unsightly, and otherwise grating to the senses. The problem has become acute with the growth of industry and population, and there is no hope whatsoever of bringing it under control except by restraint imposed by the state. Here it is particularly obvious that reason and good will and the recognition of an evil, even if universal, are of little help, and that the only hope lies in strong law vigorously enforced. The reason for this is that, however clearly someone may recognize the danger to himself and to everyone else of a certain practice—say, that of releasing large volumes of noxious gases into the air—the advantages of that practice may far outweigh the dangers *to him;* and with the likelihood that someone else will do it if he does not and thereby present those same dangers but none of the advantages, he will rush to beat his competitor. Here the state must restrain everyone from such a practice; it must be armed with the threat of heavy fines and have the power to impose them on any citizen who violates its rules. Nothing else offers the slightest hope, and no institution other than the state has the requisite power.

The nature of the common good   These three examples, which could be added to considerably, illustrate the concept of *the common good* and the need of a powerful state to protect it. The common good may be characterized as anything which is (a) of deep concern to all, (b) easily threatened by a few, and (c) in need of overwhelming power for its protection. Such power is described as *overwhelming* because it must be greater than what can be summoned by any man *or combination of men* within the state. The state, for example, must be able to protect such a good against the vast combinations of wealth and industry that are possible, for it would otherwise be reduced to vain and pathetic exhortation, and the common good would be lost in a mad scramble for private advantage.

The state as a provider of services   Besides protecting goods that are thus appropriately called common, there is another familiar realm of state activity that has nothing to do with the criminal law; it consists of the provision of *services*. These are services, not always available to all, which are nevertheless believed, rightly or wrongly, to be more effectively provided by the state than by others. Examples are: Public schooling, the construction of roads and bridges, the administration of welfare payments, underwriting the construction of low-income housing, postal services, agricultural research and the preparation of agricultural bulletins for farmers, the generation of electrical power, insurance for soldiers and the aged, provision of medical services, and so on. The list grows larger and larger as the state, with its enormous reserves, takes upon itself more and more to provide what its citizens, or large numbers of them, want. What distinguishes these state activities from the protection of the common good is that they are (a) frequently services that are performed by nongovernmental agencies as well as by government, and (b) sometimes not of deep concern to all, but only to certain groups such as farmers or veterans. Thus no agency other than the state could undertake the protection of wildlife throughout its realm with any hope of success; but nongovernmental corporations have undertaken such services as the distribution of mail, which is thought of throughout the world as a typical governmental service. In principle there is no more reason why this should be a state function than, say, the provision of telephone service. Similarly, agencies other than government do agricultual research and distribute their findings to farmers, insure veterans and the aged, produce electrical power, provide medical care, and provide schooling for children.

The justification for these governmental activities is not, therefore, that if they were not undertaken by the state there would be little hope of their being done at all, but rather, that they are thought to be done better, or more cheaply, or more efficiently, by the state than otherwise. This is, of course, sometimes a matter of deep controversy. Indeed it is the focal point of all political divisions and shades of political opinion. Hardly anyone imagines that agencies other than the state could more effectively protect the common good—that we could, for example, better entrust private agencies to settle civil suits, or to protect wildlife and other natural resources, or to maintain a healthy environment. On the other hand it can be doubted whether the state is the appropriate agency for the generation of electrical power and the provision of other services originally provided by other sources.

There is of course no general answer to this question. It varies from one service to another. Few would suggest that there should be *no* public schooling, for example, that it should be left instead to private enterprise, as it already is to some extent, or that the state should have no hand in the construction of highways, which might better be privately owned. A similar opinion is less obvious, however, when applied to medical care or the publication of useful and informative books. It is, however, clear enough, up to a point, how provision by the state of this or that service is to be justified or condemned. The justification is *not* that such state action is necessary for the protection of the common good, for it is not. The justification can be to show that such state provision is (a) cheaper, or (b) more fair, through its enablement of wider participation than would be possible otherwise, or (c) more effective, in requiring resources available only to the state.

The second of these claims can often be made out quite convincingly. Unless the state assumed a responsibility for the education of children, for example, then the children of the poor would remain ignorant, perpetuating a distinction between the privileged and the abused and exploited far greater than the considerable distinction that already exists. The claim that the state should now assume a greater role in the provision of medical care, it is worth noting, is defended on precisely this same ground, and those who oppose such a state role would seldom take the same position with respect to education. Thus it is said that unless the state assumes this responsibility, then the poor are destined to ill health, or to much more than their share of it, thereby again perpetuating a distinction of classes.

The proliferation of bureaucracy   It is the first and third of these claims in favor of state action that are most controversial—namely, that the state does these things more cheaply and effectively than private agencies or corporations. Experience repeatedly shows that governmental agencies, drawing upon virtually inexhaustible public treasuries, do nothing cheaply or efficiently. On the contrary it is a part of their very nature to spawn huge, cumbersome, and prodigiously wasteful bureaucracies. Whenever it is found that an agency is not getting something accomplished very well, the standard solution is to appoint additional personnel, then more and more endlessly, there being almost no reliable way of goading the complacent personnel already on hand to greater efficiency. This boundless waste is fairly well kept from the sight of those who pay for it, however, and even from the bureaucrat himself, since there is no requirement that performance be measured in any meaningful terms such as profit and loss. There are also always available artful but meaningless ways of creating the appearance of accomplishment, such as the endless preparation of forms and publication of reports. This accounts mainly for the awesome consumption of paper by a bureaucracy and its generation of secretarial tasks. The expenditure of energy and materials is thought of as work and identified with the achievement of ends, thus filling the bureaucrat's life with mission and concealing even from him the basic pointlessness and waste of most of what he does.

The public resentment of proliferating bureaucratic superstructures and of their ever-increasing cost is therefore not groundless. They seem indestructible and possessed of an infinite capacity for growth, so that they become a millstone to the body politic, an encumberance that cannot be dislodged, as durable as the state itself. Probably every shade of political opinion can be measured in terms of one's conception of the nature and role of governmental bureaucracy, from those who would turn with hope to government for the solution of every social ill, which inevitably means the increase of bureaucracy, to those who would sweep the whole of it away.

Summary Government, then, is justified, not by its form—that is, by its democratic or despotic character or whatever—nor by the particular relationship that it establishes between rulers and ruled. Whether those who hold political power are in some sense "chosen" by those whom they govern, and if so, how, or whether they are simply placed over them by an army, or by formal tests of hereditary inheritance of rule, or what—all these questions are important, but not philosophically so. The answers to them do not by themselves justify or invalidate a particular government. That justification or invalidation is provided by the ends or purposes pursued by the state and by its effectiveness in attaining them.

Government, then, is best thought of as an activity, rather than as a relationship between men. Like any activity, it is directed towards ends—not *an* end, but many of them. When these are good and are effectively achieved, then government is good, and its justification is apparent. When those ends are bad, then government has the same quality and is without justification, even though it might meet every test of formal rightness. The most perfect democracy, faithful to the most perfectly democratic constitution, could be the worst government imaginable in case its people were ignorant and stupid, and they elected ignorant and stupid public servants who pursued foolish goals or were inept in their pursuit of better ones. The habit among political philosophers of seeking the justification of government in formal and legalistic considerations is thus misguided and even dangerous, since these considerations tend to mislead those who formulate public policies. It actually happens, for example, that wars are fought or prolonged over such considerations because it is assumed in some quarters that a good government—of some small Asian country, for example—will be one that is democratic in form, and that whatever "falls short" of this will accordingly be less than good.

The most general end of the state is the promotion of freedom. But freedom has two forms, that of permission and that of enablement. The former is protected by a criminal law that is drafted in accordance with the principle of liberty. Essentially there is but one such law: Do not injure. The freedom of enablement, on the other hand, is promoted in two ways—by the protection of the common good and by the provision of certain services, both of which are the function of civil law. There are thus essentially two civil laws that are not expressed in the form of prohibition like the criminal law. The first of them establishes the machinery for protecting whatever is of deep concern to all from destruction by the few for private advantage; it requires nothing less than the overwhelming power of the state. The second establishes the bureaucracies through which particular services, not identical with the common good and not uniquely associated with government, are provided.

It is thus through the legal order, the criminal law on the one hand and the civil law in both aspects on the other, that human freedom becomes possible. Freedom is therefore possible only within a legal order, or which is the same thing, only within the vastly powerful state. It is generally believed, with some truth, that this possibility is best realized within a democracy; but democratic forms and procedures do not by themselves guarantee it, nor do other forms, in certain circumstances, render it unattainable. Men can, and sometimes do, live outside any legal order, as do all other creatures on earth; but when we envy such life (and even occasionally escape to it), we are taking for granted the protections and blessings of the legal order, which is seldom far away. Law is, to be sure, the invention and creation of men and therefore something men can destroy; but the human will and the need of its free expression is no creation of men. It is given to us without choice by God or nature, and until men cease to be men, they will be creatures who are governed, not at the cost of freedom, but in the name of it.

INDEX

Index

G

Goat's milk, 17, 18
God:
  duties to, 76–84
  the folly of rejecting Him, 23, 24
  His commandments, 76–84
  His goodness, 7
  His power, 6–7
  His restraints upon men, 39
  how He is proudly served by the believer, 10
  not always to be obeyed, 81–82
  as sovereign, 5–10
  the willful disobedience of Him by Adam and Eve, 23
Good:
  as an absolute, 33, 36
  as a distinction of nature, 31
  as a distinction of the will, 28–30
Government:
  as an activity, 118–22
  and divine right, 122–23
  as a human creation, 2, 20
  by laws, absurdity of, 97–98
  by majority, 106
  and morality, 67, 68, 101–3
  by the people, 105–6
  the philosophical problems of, 11, 14–15, 18–19
  as a provider of services, 133–34
  and social contract, 109–17

H

Happiness, 32–40
  and the common good, 35
  as fulfillment, 36
  and the will, 32
  and wisdom, 35

I

Idiocy, 72
Injury:
  and crime, 65, 66–67

Injury (*cont.*)
  J. S. Mill's confusions concerning, 56–60
  natural and conventional, 63
  the nature of, 61–62
  to property, 64

J

Jefferson, T., 131
Justification:
  and the ends of government, 124
  problem of, 94–100

K

Kant, I., 49
  as supreme moralist, 103

L

Law:
  civil, 130–36
  criminal, 125–29
  frivolous, 78–79
Legitimacy, 85–93
  and anarchy, 48–54
  and *de facto* political power, 91–92
  of government, 88–93
  of law, 85–89
  levels of, 87–90
  of policy, 88–92
  and political justification, 86–87
  problem of, 85
  and the recognition of foreign governments, 92–93
Liberty (*see* Freedom)
Love:
  as the basis of communal life, 44
  as the basis of family life, 43
  as the foundation of anarchy, 43

S

Salvation, how endangered by learning, 80
Satan, how he is obsequiously served by the coward, 11
Sex:
  and criminality, 67
  and liberty, 67–68
Social contract, fabulous nature of (*see* Contract)
Societies, natural and conventional, 3–4
Socrates, 113
  his conception of God's will, 25
  his conception of justice, 29
Sovereignty, 5–15
  and contract, 110–11
  over oneself, 105
  as supremacy of the will, 6–7
  what it is, 5–6
State of nature, 21

T

Theocracy, 122–23
  and communism, 122

U

Utility, as a poor basis of political justification, 103–4

W

Wolff, R., 46, 97
  his strange abstractions, 49–51

SCIENCE AND THE PARANORMAL

____ESP & Parapsychology: A Critical Re-evaluation *C.E.M. Hansel* — $9.95

____Extra-Terrestrial Intelligence *James L. Christian, editor* — 7.95

____Objections to Astrology *L. Jerome & B. Bok* — 4.95

____The Psychology of the Psychic *D. Marks & R. Kammann* — 9.95

____Philosophy & Parapsychology *J. Ludwig, editor* — 9.95

____Paranormal Borderlands of Science *Kendrick Frazier, editor* — 13.95

HUMANISM

____Ethics Without God *K. Nielsen* — 6.95

____Humanist Alternative *Paul Kurtz, editor* — 5.95

____Humanist Ethics *Morris, Storer, editor* — 9.95

____Humanist Funeral Service *Corliss Lamont* — 3.95

____Humanist Manifestos I & II — 1.95

____Humanist Wedding Service *Corliss Lamont* — 2.95

____Humanistic Psychology *Welch, Tate, Richards, editors* — 10.95

____Moral Problems in Contemporary Society *Paul Kurtz, editor* — 7.95

____Voice in the Wilderness *Corliss Lamont* — 5.95

____A Secular Humanist Declaration — 1.95

LIBRARY OF LIBERAL RELIGION

____Facing Death and Grief *George N. Marshall* — 7.95

____Living Religions of the World *Carl Hermann Voss* — 4.95

PHILOSOPHY & ETHICS

____Art of Deception *Nicholas Capaldi* — 6.95

____Beneficent Euthanasia *M. Kohl, editor* — 8.95

____Esthetics Contemporary *Richard Kostelanetz, editor* — 11.95

____Exuberance A Philosophy of Happiness *Paul Kurtz* — 3.00

____Fullness of Life *Paul Kurtz* — 6.95

____Freedom of Choice Affirmed *Corliss Lamont* — 4.95

____Humanhood: Essays in Biomedical Ethics *Joseph Fletcher* — 8.95

____Journeys Through Philosophy *N. Capaldi & L. Navia, editors* — 14.95

____Philosophy: An Introduction *Antony Flew* — 6.95

____Thinking Straight *Antony Flew* — 5.95

____Worlds of Plato & Aristotle *Wilbur & Allen, editors* — 7.95

____Worlds of the Early Greek Philosophers *Wilbur & Allen, editors* — 8.95

____Animal Rights and Human Morality *Bernard Rollin* — 9.95

____A Secular Humanist Declaration *drafted by Paul Kurtz* — **1.95**

____Worlds of Hume and Kant *Wilbur & Allen, editors* — 7.95

____Problem of God *Peter A. Angeles* — 9.95

____Invitation to Philosophy *Capaldi, Kelly, Navia, editors* — 12.95

____Infanticide and the Value of Life *Marvin Kohl, editor* — 8.95

____Responsibilities to Future Generations *Ernest Partridge, editor* — 9.95

____Reverse Discrimination *Barry Gross, editor* — 9.95

____Introductory Readings in the Philosophy of Science *Klemke, Hollinger, Kline, editors* — 12.95

____Ethics and the Search for Values *L. Navia and E. Kelly, editors* — 13.95

SEXOLOGY

_____The Frontiers of Sex Research *Vern Bullough, editor*   8.95

_____New Bill of Sexual Rights & Responsibilities *Lester Kirkendall*   3.95

_____New Sexual Revolution *Lester Kirkendall, editor*   6.95

_____Philosophy & Sex *Robert Baker & Fred Elliston, editors*   7.95

_____Sex Without Love: A Philosophical Exploration *Russell Vannoy*   8.95

                                                                                9.95

THE SKEPTIC'S BOOKSHELF

_____Classics of Free Thought *Paul Blanshard, editor*   6.95

_____Critiques of God *Peter Angeles, editor*   9.95

_____What About Gods? (for children) *Chris Brockman*   4.95

_____Atheism: The Case Against God *George H. Smith*   7.95

_____Atheist Debater's Handbook *B.C. Johnson*   10.95

SOCIAL ISSUES

_____Age of Aging: A Reader in Social Gerontology *Monk, editor*   9.95

The books listed above can be obtained from your book dealer
or directly from Prometheus Books.
Please check off the appropriate books.
Remittance must accompany all orders from individuals.
Please include $1.50 postage and handling for first book,
.50 for each additional book ($4.00 maximum).
(N.Y. State Residents add 7% sales tax)

Send to _____

(Please type or print clearly)

Address _____

City _____ State_____ Zip_____

(Prices subject to change without notice)

Amount Enclosed_____

Prometheus Books
700 E. Amherst St.
Buffalo, New York 14215